To Luis,
To teach c[...]

PRIVATE LESSONS

Jay Jones

PRIVATE LESSONS

A BOOK OF
MEDITATIONS FOR TEACHERS

JOY JONES

**Andrews McMeel
Publishing**

Kansas City

01 02 03 04 05 MVP 10 9 8 7 6 5 4 3 2 1

Library of Congress Cataloging-in-Publication Data
Jones, Joy.
    Private lessons : meditations for teachers / Joy Jones.
        p. cm.
    ISBN 0-7407-1875-4
    1. Teachers—Miscellanea. 2. Quotations. I. Title.

LB1775 .J56 2001
371.1—dc2

2001046324

Book design and composition by Holly Camerlinck

────────── **Attention: Schools and Businesses** ──────────

Andrews McMeel books are available at quantity discounts with bulk purchase for educational, business, or sales promotional use. For information, please write to: Special Sales Department, Andrews McMeel Publishing, 4520 Main Street, Kansas City, Missouri 64111.

To my most important teachers:

my mother,
Marilyn Francis Jones

and the memory of my grandmother,
Nannie Mae Powell

ACKNOWLEDGMENTS

Thanks, praise, and appreciation to:

My favorite teachers:
Celia Dunn, Delores Burnett, Lou Slyker, and Judith Tydings.

Favorite people who happen to be teachers:
Eunice Wright Jones, Mary Thomas Newsom, Bob Newsom, Jennifer Gibbs-Phillips, Deborah Menkart, S. Michele Rucker, Russell Nesbit, and Nancy Schwalb.

Those who are not teachers, but who have taught me a lot:
Lorraine Jones, Vita Washington, W. Morgan Jones, Jackie Grice, Tom Adams, Darnell Yelder, Doris Beverlin, Stephen Parham, Ann Shelton, Linda Powell, Kathy Acosta, and Robert "Buster" Washington III.

Thanks also to:
Wanda Akin, Angeli Rasbury, Lynn Vance, Yvette Napper, Dr. Jevoner Adams, Gina Masterson, Laura Brown, David Freund, Wendy Blair, Jeff Canady, Phil Kurata's Writers Group, Karibu Books, SisterSpace and Books, Black Women Playwrights Group, D.C. WritersCorps, Kramer Middle School, Backus Middle School, Fillmore Arts Center, and the Writer's Center of Bethesda, Maryland.

INTRODUCTION

On some days, simply counting to ten was not going to be enough. The rebellious student, the bureaucratic administrator, school system politics—it was enough to give even the most dedicated educator a headache, a heart attack, or at the least, a strong urge to go compulsive shopping. Don't get me wrong—I love my work; the jobs I've had in education have been the most satisfying I've ever held. But it has required me to stay on my toes intellectually, emotionally, and spiritually.

I used to keep two different pocket-sized meditation books in my desk to help me gain perspective on work concerns and personal issues. Sometimes I'd write furiously in my journal to examine my feelings about what was going on. It is out of that experience that the seed for *Private Lessons: Meditations for Teachers* was generated.

These reflections can be read in the order that they appear, from beginning to end, or you may choose to play "meditation roulette"— open the book at random and see what is revealed. At the end of the book are a few blank pages headed with thought-provoking quotations so that you can write down thoughts of your own. If you'd like to share them with me, send them to: Joy Jones, P.O. Box 29316, Washington, DC 20017, or visit me on the Web at www.joyjonesonline.com.

Teaching is creative, demanding work. To do it right you have to give a lot. However, even the most generous givers need to receive now and then. The best gift you can give yourself is the occasion to think, reflect, and quietly take in the lessons of life. It is my hope that *Private Lessons* gives you that occasion.

ACTION

The truth of the matter is that you always know the right thing to do.
The hard part is doing it.

—GENERAL H. NORMAN SCHWARZKOPF

The music teacher was the new teacher in the school. She didn't know that Reggie was one of the "knuckleheads," but she soon found out. He had a chip on his shoulder, and he was sullen and unresponsive in her music appreciation class. She took the time to talk to Reggie and found out that he was having a lot of problems at home—a mother struggling to get off drugs, a father who lived in another state whom he missed sorely, a big sister who was serving a jail term, and his own curiosity about the excitement of street life. By talking with Reggie on a regular basis she helped him to drop—by degrees—his hard edge. Almost in spite of himself, he began to like music class—so much so, he decided to take up playing the trumpet. Soon he was a member of the band. Then as school began to be more fun as a result of music class, he began to do better in all his other subjects, too.

One day the English teacher stopped the music teacher in the hall. "Reggie was an absolute hellion last school year. He is doing so much better now," the English teacher said to her colleague. "And it's all because you took an interest in him."

"That's true," said the music teacher. *"But why didn't you?"*

TODAY'S LESSON:

I take a personal interest in those around me.

INSTRUCTION

Why is it that nobody wants to sit in the front of the room?

I taught an adult education class. At the first session, I told my students that studies show that the people who sit in the front consistently earn higher grades. The following day, every seat on the front row was occupied. Not only that, a few students took exception to the fact that all the front seats were taken, preventing them from being able to take advantage of the proximity effect.

That made me think. It might be good to deliberately change the seating plan from time to time during the course of the term, instead of forcing the students to stay in one position the whole year. And maybe I shouldn't position myself only in front of the classroom. Maybe I needed to change my position, too.

TODAY'S LESSON:

I can change my position if it will enhance learning.

INTEGRITY

The nice thing about egotists is that they don't talk about other people.

—LUCILLE S. HARPER

"Did you hear who Edna is sleeping with?"
"Yeah, but I can't imagine what he sees in her."

"That boy Marshall is headed straight for prison—is he in your class? Boy, do I feel sorry for you."

"I hope Anita stays home from school today. These kids don't want to learn and I don't want to teach them."

3

The teachers' lounge is the place to hear all the gossip, haul all the garbage, and dish all the dirt. We cast aspersions on the administration, complain about the kids, and spread rumors about other teachers.

A little bit of steam-releasing is to be expected. But the teachers' lounge shouldn't be an insult gallery. We don't need to down-rate, denigrate, or castigate others be they children or colleagues. As the old proverb tells us: Smart people talk about ideas. Average people talk about events. Small people talk about each other.

TODAY'S LESSON:

I do not listen to or repeat gossip. I can say something positive about another person.

ENDURANCE

You may have to fight a battle more than once to win it.

—MARGARET THATCHER

Teaching is work. Sometimes going into that classroom each day is more than work, it's war. We have to cajole stubborn students to learn, pressure rigid administrators to relax the rules, persuade parents into supporting their own children. And we have to do it every day.

We get tired. We get frustrated. We suffer from combat fatigue.

But the war is not over until we win. When we're doing the right thing, we have to keep on doing it. The minds and hearts of children are at stake.

TODAY'S LESSON:

I do not get weary of doing the right thing.

PEACE

A soft answer turns away wrath.

—PROVERBS 15:1

Lynn was disliked by every member of the fourth grade and I wasn't too fond of her myself. As the substitute teacher, I was there only for the day but I wasn't sure if I was going to make it without throttling her. When she threw her notebook at me, I grabbed her by the arm and marched her down to the principal's office.

Mr. Foster saw the sullen expression on Lynn's face and the steam spewing out of my ears as we approached him. He didn't appear alarmed, didn't scold Lynn or lecture me. Mr. Foster simply invited us to sit down, as if we were guests in his living room, rather than two very angry and upset people. He spoke in a quiet, modulated voice. Somehow, his peaceful presence calmed me, helped to dissipate my anger. Even Lynn softened and became more tractable.

It taught me the value of modeling calm. A peaceful spirit can be contagious. Does your workplace need an outbreak of rampant serenity?

5

TODAY'S LESSON:

Today, I am an instrument of peace.

INSTRUCTION

Talk to anyone about himself and he will listen without interrupting.

—HERBERT V. PROCHNOW

I taught a creative writing class to elementary school students, but most of the creativity came in trying to convince them to write. Yet by the end of the school year, I had managed to collect enough of their poems to print an anthology. When the books were passed out, all of a sudden everybody got excited about writing. The work became more meaningful when they saw their words in print.

The next term I worked with most of those same children in the creative writing class. Once again, I often found it hard to keep their attention. One day, I flipped open last year's anthology to show them an example of the kinds of poem I wanted them to write. The students gazed at the pages as if I had presented the Holy Writ—their very own work was being used as a textbook! Their very own words were being used as an example of what was right.

The children whose poetry I cited were elevated to the status of celebrities. Their interest in the assignment increased a thousandfold— by geometric proportions. Discipline problems dissolved that day when they saw themselves in the lesson.

TODAY'S LESSON:

I make the student the focus of my attention.

FAITH

On my underground railroad I never ran my train off the track.
And I never lost a passenger.

—HARRIET TUBMAN

Harriet Tubman was a slave who craved freedom. Not waiting for anyone to hand it to her, she freed herself by escaping from the plantation on foot and establishing herself up North. But freedom for herself only and not for her brothers and sisters was not enough. Tubman made nineteen dangerous journeys back to the South and led three hundred more slaves to freedom, including her elderly parents.

Despite bounty hunters, traitors, and double-minded slaves, she credits her faith and trust in God for allowing her to keep her "train" from running off the track. She told escaping slaves who entertained second thoughts that there was absolutely no turning back. Once they were one of her "passengers" they were committed to freedom.

Our students are passengers on the train whose destination is knowledge. Are we determined to stay on track and leave no child back? Do we believe all children can learn? Or do we figure it's okay to lose a few? Do we have sufficient faith to motivate others to keep moving forward despite their fears? If not, are we willing to cultivate that kind of faith?

TODAY'S LESSON:

I have faith.

INTEGRITY

I'd rather fail trying to do something great than to do nothing and succeed.

—ROBERT SCHULLER

One way of believing you could have been an A student is to never turn in your homework. That way, you think that had you actually completed your homework, you would have done it well—but since you didn't, and no one will ever know . . . why not assume it would have been an A paper?

One way of believing you could have played in the NBA is to drop out of school. That way, you think that had you actually gone to college, a recruiter would have snapped you up because you would have been such a star on the court—but since you didn't finish college, and no one can say what would have happened anyway, well . . . why not believe you would have played pro ball?

When we hear our students say these things, we recognize the words for what they are—excuses. Pitiful, self-serving, ego-saving deceptions used to avoid taking the chance, doing the work, facing the challenge. Whether the playing field of confrontation is a classroom, boardroom, or office, once you step on the field, you'll have to fight the good fight and maybe even lose. You'll find out what your strengths and weaknesses are—and you won't find out by sitting in an easy chair and reading about them in a book, but by having your qualities put to an actual test. Yet even if you fall short, you can still stand tall because the experience will stretch you and make you grow.

TODAY'S LESSON:
Nothing stops me from doing my best as a teacher.

GROWTH

If dandelions were hard to grow, they would be most welcome on any lawn.

—ANDREW V. MASON

Oh no! The principal put all the worst behavior problems in your class. You won't have a minute's rest all year with those loudmouthed, disrespectful, refusing-to-learn hardheads. It's unfair. "Why should I be given such a trying group to work with?" you think angrily.

That's one way to look at it. There's another point of view. Here's a chance to try something new. Even small progress with such a group will be regarded as a victory. This might be the case where you can make a name for yourself. If you can't change the situation, change your attitude.

9

TODAY'S LESSON:
I rise to the challenge.

INSTRUCTION

I am 83 years old and I have come to realize that there is always
more in life to learn. I just started taking swimming lessons last year.
I ask a lot of questions during my swimming lessons. You can drown yourself
with problems if you do not ask questions.

—ROSA PARKS

You may be the teacher but you are still in the position of learner. To be in the position of a learner is to be in a humble position. One definition of humility is to be teachable. When you acknowledge that you are the student, you are admitting that there are things that you don't know.

We never get to the place where we don't need to learn—even in our areas of expertise. We may have been teaching third grade for thirty years, we may be the head of the department or have a Ph.D. in our subject, but we still lack lots and lots of information on the very subject we genuinely know a great deal about.

It may be time to update the lesson that hasn't changed in years. Perhaps there is a different way of presenting the material we're so familiar with. Is there a new skill we should acquire that will improve our instructional delivery? More than likely the answer is yes.

TODAY'S LESSON:

I still have a lot to learn.

DISCIPLINE

People are nothing but a bunch of walking habits.

—NANNIE MAE POWELL

What kind of habits do you have? Is your free time spent in couch-potato land? Is your curriculum the same one you've taught for the last ten years?

The student who reviews her notes on a regular basis is the student most likely to pass the test. The basketball player who practices layups every afternoon is more likely to be the player who makes the shot during the game. The writer who makes a habit of spending time in front of the computer every day is the writer most likely to complete a book. To a significant extent, success is due not to outstanding talent or great luck, but to the practice of good work routines.

Our own work can be improved by cultivating helpful habits and eliminating harmful ones.

TODAY'S LESSON:

I will cultivate one new good habit.

DRESS

Mirror, Mirror on the wall, I don't want to hear one word out of you.

—JEAN KERR

Experts say that the people who aspire to get promoted begin to communicate that aspiration by dressing like the boss. They come to work wearing the kinds of clothes the manager, the CEO, the district superintendent wears. Others begin to see them in the role of supervisor because they already look the part.

What message does your clothing convey to your superiors or to your students: I'm satisfied right where I am; I don't care; I'm ready to move up.

TODAY'S LESSON:

I dress for success.

LOVE

Love always sees more than is in evidence at any moment of viewing.

—HOWARD THURMAN

Remember when you first fell in love? The excitement, joy, and drama of it all. When we love someone we tend to view them with rose-colored glasses. "He's such a sensitive and caring person." "She's unique; so different from anyone I've ever met."

Remember when you first decided to teach? How marvelous you believed it would be to work with fresh eager minds, how stimulating to have conversations about pedagogy and academic issues with other educators. How proud you would be to call yourself a teacher.

Chances are, you no longer feel that way. Now you probably regard those days as dazed, distorted thinking, similar to the early stage of a love affair when love is blind. But although in one sense, love is blind, love also opens one's eyes to an alternate reality. When we are influenced by love, we see with an expanded, exalted point of view. With love, we are able to see the good in others though it be hidden. With love, we are motivated to extend ourselves for our beloved's benefit. With love, we are able to believe in a student's potential, even when that student doesn't believe it exists. When we love, seeing is believing.

TODAY'S LESSON:

I teach my class in a spirit of love.

INTUITION

There's a part of me that I didn't even realize I had until recently—instinct, intuition, whatever. It helps me and protects me. It's perceptive and astute. I just listen to the inside of me and I know what to do.

—WOMAN QUOTED IN <u>WOMEN'S WAYS OF KNOWING,</u> BY MARY FIELD BELENKY, BLYTHE MCVICKER CLINCHY, NANCY RULE GOLDBERGER, AND JILL MATTUCK TARULE

14

I know that I know
Though no one told me so.
I know but can't explain.
I understand, but not by my brain.
What wonders will come to fruition
If I honor my intuition?

TODAY'S LESSON:

I look for an intuitive prompt to help me solve my problems.

MONEY

Mamma may have
Poppa may have
But God bless the child that's got his own
That's got his own.

—BILLIE HOLIDAY

"How crass," thought Sheila, when she heard that her pregnant coworker had strongly hinted that gifts of cash were preferred at the baby shower. The mother established a bank account for her daughter upon her birth and deposited the checks that were her baby gifts. For each holiday, birthday, or special occasion thereafter, the mother again encouraged donations of money. Some of the baby's family members gave very modest gifts, $5, $10, even a roll of coins—all of which were put in the baby's bank account.

When the girl reached age four, Sheila realized that this baby had more in savings than *she* did—and Sheila was working every day while the baby had never held a job in her life. Then Sheila began to see the wisdom of establishing a bank account for the child instead of buying playthings. For a preschooler, designer clothes and fancy toys mean nothing. They grow out of the clothes faster than they could ever wear them out and they quickly lose interest in the toys if they don't lose the actual toys.

But the savings account was something that would benefit the child more than any clever computer game or cute ruffled dress. What was true for the preschooler was also true for the professional—it would be more prudent and profitable to make saving the priority.

Now, every payday, Sheila pays herself first.

TODAY'S LESSON:

Pay yourself first.

RESPECT

If you thought being a student was hard, try being a teacher.

—AD FOR THE TV SHOW <u>BOSTON PUBLIC</u>

I once read about an exchange program between corporation executives and school principals. The executives spent the day handling behavior problems, taking over classes that had an absent teacher, talking to parents. The principals spent their day touring the premises, attending luncheon meetings, and playing with the latest computer equipment. The principals had a thoroughly enjoyable workday. The executives reported that they were exhausted by three o'clock.

Before the switch, I'm sure that some of those executives probably thought that a job in education was a cross between an amusement park and a library—you played all day and read books. But they found out otherwise. It's mentally demanding and emotionally taxing. Teachers don't get three-martini lunches, expense accounts, or even a telephone on the desk.

Even if the world doesn't always acknowledge it, we know we are champions. We need to carry ourselves as the heroes we know ourselves to be.

TODAY'S LESSON:

My work is worthy of respect.

COURTESY

When you pass on the blessings, you become a magnet for more and more to flow to you.

—PATTI LABELLE

The best school I worked for impressed me the first day. The secretary was friendly and helpful. The principal greeted me as a colleague and didn't act as if she was so busy or important that she didn't have time to talk with me. If there were changes in the schedule or a program, I was notified in advance, not expected to shift gears in the middle of a change and adapt as best I could. This had not been my usual experience. Of course, they also expected more from me and I found I was willing to give more.

Courtesy and consideration are as effective as rudeness and resentment in starting a chain reaction. Why not be the catalyst for a courtesy explosion at your school?

TODAY'S LESSON:

I will go out of my way to show courtesy.

INSTRUCTION

Wanting to work is so rare a want that it should be encouraged.

—ABRAHAM LINCOLN

Many businesses offer a "frequent buyers" club. Those customers who spend a lot of money or spend money often are rewarded with discounts, free gifts, or special offers. That makes sense. How would it seem if companies rewarded their best customers with more work, higher prices, or fewer services?

But that's sometimes how we treat our best pupils. Those who finish one assignment quickly find that they are given more work to do. The child who is obedient and does her work without a lot of supervision often gets little or no teacher attention, feedback, or guidance.

Offer a little customer appreciation to your class. Reward the swift student by giving him first choice for a classroom privilege. Be certain to encourage and compliment the quiet girl who's working alone. Make sure you praise good behavior just as you punish bad behavior.

TODAY'S LESSON:

I support and reward good behavior.

SERVICE

Love involves a willingness to suffer and be inconvenienced.

—LEWIS F. PRESNALL

Every now and then you need to do something foolish. No, not something silly or embarrassing. Not fun or funny although there is a time and place for that, too. By foolish, I mean performing an act of strategic insanity. This is a situation when you do a good deed on another's behalf, even though the odds are that they won't change their behavior, appreciate the gesture, or accept the gift.

So, occasionally give a mischievous child the benefit of the doubt, compliment the grouchy administrator, do a favor for your ungrateful neighbor, offer some money to the panhandler and hope he doesn't spend it on drugs. It's not wise to make these gestures compulsively; it's not something to do all the time or even most of the time. It may be a complete waste of time.

But you never know.

TODAY'S LESSON:

I am of service to others.

GROWTH

When I got my library card, that's when my life began.

—RITA MAE BROWN

Readers are leaders and leaders are readers. How many times have you told your students this one? How often do you practice it yourself?

I don't just mean pleasure reading. Have you kept up with the latest books in your subject area?

I attended a conference where one of the day's sessions was to sit and read quietly. The workshop leader brought in many of the latest titles in the educational field and invited teachers to browse, pick one book, and catch up on their professional reading.

It's trickier to be able to do that in one's everyday life but it can be done. You may not be able to commit to a whole hour, but you could carve out fifteen minutes to read several times a week.

TODAY'S LESSON:
I make time to sit quietly and read.

EQUITY

Boy: A noise with some dirt on it.

—MITZI CHANDLER

Boys are boys. They are loud, withdrawn, gregarious, and nefarious. We like them better than the girls. We don't like them much at all. Boys are discipline problems and they try our patience. They astonish us with their brilliant ideas and open minds. They give us plenty to complain about in the teachers' lounge. They are the source of our funniest stories when we talk about our work.

Thousands of boys are born each year and it seems like the worst trouble-makers of each year's crop seem to wind up in your classroom. Boys—they are fun, they are frustrating, and they are the people you have pledged to educate.

TODAY'S LESSON:

I appreciate the boys I teach.

EQUITY

The most exciting thing about women's liberation is that this century will be able to take advantage of talent and potential genius that have been wasted because of taboos.

—HELEN REDDY

Girls are easy to teach. They sit quietly at their desks and do their seat work. They are eager to volunteer and help out. Their handwriting is neater and easier to read. Girls are more willing to please, more suited to the classroom environment than boys. They cause less trouble.

Because of these qualities girls are harder to teach because they're easier to overlook. We need to make a concerted effort not to let the compliant nature of the female students be the quiet backdrop in the class while we are busy meting out discipline for or finding new ways to challenge the boys in the room. It's tempting to feel grateful that the girls are not as demanding on our energies so we may ignore them and their academic needs.

Of course, not all girls are quiet, compliant, and nonchallenging, either. Some girls think they are as grown as the teacher. They can be aggressive and smart-mouthed.

Girls are treasures, they are troublemakers. They have sharp, scientific minds. They drop out of school by the dozens, hundreds, thousands each year. They make teaching worthwhile and at times they make teaching seem more trouble than it's worth. Every girl in my classroom deserves the height of my skill and the focus of my attention.

Every day.

TODAY'S LESSON:

I give attention and care to the girls I teach.

RESPECT

Nobody can do everything, but everybody can do something and if everybody does something, everything will get done.

—GIL SCOTT-HERON

Holidays, holy days, and special commemorative months are times for school celebrations to honor great men and women from the past. And it is fitting that we do so. But we must also remember to honor and acknowledge the men and women in our daily lives; the ordinary people who laugh and weep with us, who get on our nerves and who give us delight. The people who impact on our personal lives in a way no historical figure or successful celebrity ever could. When we reflect on the contributions of the well known, let us also reflect on ways to say "I thank you," "I love you," or just "I see you" to those close to home. To paraphrase the Bible, how can we say that we love, honor, and respect heroes and "sheroes" whom we have never seen when we do not love, honor, or respect the brothers and sisters whom we see daily?

Every person is a Very Important Person, whether or not his or her name hits the headlines or is recorded in the history books. Everyone's contribution is special. More than that, everybody's life is necessary, indispensable, vital. That which is ordinary is sacred and absolutely crucial to everybody's success.

TODAY'S LESSON:

I acknowledge and respect each one who crosses my path.

PATIENCE

What gives light must endure burning.

—VIKTOR FRANKL

"Why do I have to keep raising my voice?"
"Boys and girls, please sit down and listen!"
"Yes, we have to go over this again and again until you learn it."

A lightbulb. A candle. A log in a fireplace. A teacher. All these things bring illumination. We illuminate our students' minds via knowledge. A noble task, but ah, a tedious one. When we see that "Aha" spark in a child's eyes, it makes our hearts leap. But those brilliant moments flash fleetingly between dark tunnels of grading papers, behavior problems, a broken telephone in the teachers' lounge, rationing of paper for the photocopier, a school secretary who has perpetual PMS, a principal whose real name must be Hitler, a bureaucratic, uncaring central administration, repetitive paperwork, negative reports in the press about the school system—then it's the second day of school and you get to face more of the same. Then one day midsemester you see that Tina "got it." Something clicked on in her mind and you saw that she understood the lesson it took such pains to teach.

It took all that preceded for this illuminating moment to happen. And yes, it was worth it.

TODAY'S LESSON:

I am patient with the learning process.

INSTRUCTION

The effective teacher starts the class immediately with an assignment, not roll taking.

—HARRY K. WONG AND ROSEMARY T. WONG

"Don't waste time taking roll," I was told. *That's not a waste of time* was my first reaction. Recording attendance is important, but there is no need to spend a lot of time on this routine task when there are numerous easy, unobtrusive ways to check who's in and who isn't. A seating chart, a sign-in sheet, a silent glance about the room as students are doing seat work are all more efficient ways to note attendance.

When we don't spend time taking roll, that leaves more time to spend teaching.

25

TODAY'S LESSON:

I maximize the time for teaching.

OPPORTUNITY

I don't know anything about luck. I've never banked on it, and I'm afraid of people who do. Luck, for me is something else; hard work and realizing what is opportunity and what isn't.

—LUCILLE BALL

Robert Augustus Chesebrough saw the handwriting on the wall, and the word was bankruptcy. He was a chemist who sold kerosene, and in 1859, petroleum fuel was becoming more popular than kerosene, plus it was cheaper. Chesebrough decided to go to Titusville, Pennsylvania, where there was an oil strike, to learn about the petroleum business. While there, he noticed that the drills often got clogged by a sticky, waxy residue. Work had to be stopped frequently to clean the detested paraffinlike gunk from the equipment.

Chesebrough decided to examine this petroleum waste product in his laboratory. Workers at the oil field had accidentally discovered that the jelly had a healing effect when applied to burns. Using himself as a guinea pig, Chesebrough found that this paste was very effective for speedy healing without infection. By 1870, he had a new product to present to the world, Vaseline petroleum jelly.

In the hands of one who was curious and industrious, what began as a waste product became a formula for success.

TODAY'S LESSON:

I seize the opportunity that is before me.

GOAL SETTING

With your hands you make your success, with your hands you destroy success.

—YORUBA PROVERB

A lesson plan usually starts with an objective and is followed by tasks that will help the learner gain mastery of the concept. You take the time necessary to develop a lesson plan for understanding the properties of hydrogen gas or for memorizing multiplication tables but what plan have you made for accomplishing the tasks of your own life?

Think back to what you were doing five years ago. Imagine someone had questioned you then about what you would be doing today—are you where you anticipated you would be? What were your hopes and dreams for the coming five years? Have any of them materialized?

Five more years are going to pass. What would you like to be doing by then? Now is the time to write a "lesson plan" for your goals. Get them down on paper and mark the timetable on a calendar. Decide what small tasks you need to do in order to meet the big objective.

TODAY'S LESSON:

I write down the tasks I need to do to achieve my goals.

SUCCESS

Success is more a function of consistent common sense than it is of genius.

—AN WANG

The difference between success and failure is the same as the difference between intelligence and ignorance. It's the ability to make skillful choices. Consider the root meanings of intelligence and ignorance. "Intell" is the Latin root that means "between" and "lego" means "to choose." An intelligent person is one who knows when to say yes and when to say no—who, as the song puts it, "knows when to hold 'em, knows when to fold 'em, knows when to walk away and knows when to run."

Ignorance is normally defined as lacking knowledge. But ignorance can also be characterized as ignoring—choosing not to look at something, to disregard available knowledge, to not pay attention.

What are you ignoring? What piece of information are you overlooking?

TODAY'S LESSON:

I am aware.

LISTENING

The dictum that great wisdom comes from the "mouths of babes"
is recognized as an absolute fact by anyone who truly listens to children.

—M. SCOTT PECK

"Be quiet!"
  "Stop talking."
  "Don't speak when I'm speaking."

We constantly exhort children to listen to us. Do we ever listen to what the children are saying? If we attend to what children say we are amazed at the valuable insights that come forth. Sometimes their wisdom comes from stating the obvious truth, which adults are too sophisticated or embarrassed to acknowledge. Sometimes they offer an unexpected twist on how to interpret a situation. Other times they are just plain hilarious in their observations.

Give yourself a gift today. Listen to a child speak.

TODAY'S LESSON:

I listen to children.

FAITH

Although the world is full of suffering, it is full also of the overcoming of it.

—HELEN KELLER

Sometimes it seems so overwhelming—the senseless violent act reported in the morning headlines, which is followed by the major tragedy broadcast on the evening news. Not that we have to turn to the television or newspaper to hear about people in trouble. There are plenty of troubled youngsters in our schools. The fourth grader who can't get over the fact that Daddy's moved out. The teen girl with a new baby who has special needs. A boy who thinks dropping out will solve his problems.

But there are rays of hope. The teen father who continues to come to school even though he has to go to work, too. The student who is behind in her assignments but is working hard to catch up. The child who resists the temptation to use drugs although all her friends indulge.

Let us not overlook the ones who are trying to beat the odds. Our empathy and attentiveness to these children could prove to be a crucial element in how their circumstances turn out. We can be part of the positive force that tips the scales to the winning side.

TODAY'S LESSON:

I am a catalyst for hope.

KNOWLEDGE

The teacher, whether mother, priest or schoolmaster is the real maker of history.

—H. G. WELLS

Anna Stokely had lost her husband but she wasn't about to lose her farm. After her husband's death, she was faced with nine children to feed and no breadwinner. But she meant to hold her ground, literally—no small feat for a Tennessee widow during the latter part of the nineteenth century. Anna Stokely knew that a good education was important. She decided that her five sons should attend college.

She had her oldest son spend a year managing the farm, then she sent him to Wake Forest to get higher learning. While he was in school, she had her second son run the farm until it was time for him to go to college, whereupon the first son returned to resume running the farm. She did this with each son in turn. Their university experience, coupled with their farming skills, gave the boys the broadness of vision to recognize that there was a market for canning the crops they grew. In 1898, Anna Stokely and her sons established a cannery. Soon after, Stokely Foods became a major national food packer.

TODAY'S LESSON:

Education makes a difference.

EFFORT

Next to the originator of a great quote is the first quoter of it.

—RALPH WALDO EMERSON

The Ph.D. delivered a terrific speech at the teachers' convention. Her remarks about what was wrong in education and what was needed to put it right hit home. A member of the audience stood and asked the speaker to come and repeat her insights to the students at her school.

"I will not," replied the speaker. "You do it."

"Oh, but no one can say it as eloquently as you," the teacher said.

"If I were here telling a dirty joke or doing the latest dance, you'd be able to repeat it easily," said the speaker. "In fact, you'd add your own personal twist to it and make it even better. Do the same thing with the information I just gave you."

TODAY'S LESSON:

I have everything it takes to do the job.

FAITH

On the spiritual journey, the longer you go, the easier it gets and the harder it is.

—DORIS BEVERLIN

I must have eyes in the back of my head because I can see what I should have done in the past so very clearly now. Those insights weren't available to me when I was in the midst of the events of my life that have already come and gone, but they can help me navigate the territory I am currently trying to traverse. If only I knew then what I know now . . . But what I know now can help me make fewer mistakes as I go forward.

TODAY'S LESSON:

I keep learning and I keep going forward.

PERSEVERANCE

A small daily task, if it be really daily, will beat the labors of a spasmodic Hercules.

—ANTHONY TROLLOPE

When the school year begins, the students in our class come to us with just a morsel of information about a subject area. But slowly, lesson by lesson, chapter by chapter, they build upon each piece of data we present until by semester's end, they have digested a full body of knowledge.

There's an old joke—how do you eat an elephant? One bite at a time. We may have a difficult job in front of us, an elephant-sized problem staring us in the face. How will we attack it? The same way we teach negative numbers, geography class, or eat an elephant. One bite at a time.

TODAY'S LESSON:

I will work on my problems bit by bit.

COMMUNICATION

There are worse things in life than death.
Have you ever spent an evening with an insurance salesman?

—WOODY ALLEN

It's not enough to have content knowledge when you step into a class-room. Being knowledgeable about quadratic equations or Civil War battles without having good communication skills is like having a gun and shooting blindfolded. Yes, you'll hit something, although probably not the target. In a similar way, in a dull lecture some students will learn something. But you'll miss the mark with most of them.

It's ironic how when we were students we complained about the professors who droned on and on in the lecture hall and made an hour of class feel like an eon of yawns. Yet, when it's our turn to stand before a class, we too often become the same sort of informational vending machine—dispensing facts but without much animation.

TODAY'S LESSON:
I speak with enthusiasm.

ACTION

Those who can, teach.

—ANONYMOUS

Teaching is an art in itself. Too many think that only those people who can't do a thing well bother to become teachers. Not true. Actually, effective teachers are those who are fluent at two crafts—the subject itself and the craft of instructing others in its practice. After all, you have to know how to do a thing first, before you can show someone else how to do it, too.

Haven't you ever sat through a lecture by an esteemed expert who obviously knew a great deal about his discipline but who put everybody in a coma with his boring presentation? The expert was knowledgeable but had no skill in conveying it to others. So in a way, the expert's knowledge was sterile, unable to come to life and grow in another's mind. If we mean to be good teachers, we must be midwives to knowledge: able to bring it to fruition not just for ourselves but also for someone else.

Teachers can do *and* teach. We can both show and tell.

TODAY'S LESSON:

Just like any other artist, I practice and polish
the art and craft of teaching.

WISDOM

Who is wise? He who learns from all men.

—TALMUD, <u>SAYINGS OF THE FATHERS</u>

Teachers live in the best of all worlds. We don't inhabit a workplace full of nothing but men in gray flannel suits. We work with young people who exude an unfettered freshness. Their vitality keeps us flexible in our thinking. We work with our peers, people our own age who share our sentiments and sensibilities. And usually there are staff members who are veterans—men and women older than we are who have the knowledge that comes with age.

Teachers get the benefit of the philosophy and perspective of the whole human race.

TODAY'S LESSON:

I appreciate people of all ages.

PERSEVERANCE

I'm extraordinarily patient provided I get my own way in the end.

—MARGARET THATCHER

Madam C. J. Walker started life as Sarah Breedlove, a poor black girl in Louisiana. By age fourteen, she had been orphaned, gotten married, and was working as a sharecropper on a cotton field. By age twenty-two she was a mother and a widow as a result of her husband's being killed by a lynch mob.

Nevertheless, she became a wealthy businesswoman. She earned her wealth by developing hair treatments for black women. Not only did she invent a new beauty product, but she effectively marketed it and developed the careers of many other African American women who worked for her enterprise.

Yet as accomplished and as wealthy as she was, Madam C. J. Walker was not readily welcomed into the business world by her male peers. At the 1912 National Negro Business League convention, she was refused permission to address the assembly. Undaunted, she forced her way to the platform and told her story anyway.

At the 1913 National Negro Business League convention, she was one of the official presenters.

By 1914, she was the first woman in America to become a millionaire—not by inheriting money or by marrying money but by her own effort and ingenuity.

TODAY'S LESSON:

I do what it takes.

RELAXATION

The sky is the daily bread for the eyes.

—RALPH WALDO EMERSON

One of the best inventions in education is outdoor recess. Children escape the confines of the classroom to go outside, play, and release some steam. It's good to have a school building that provides shelter and protection from the elements, but it's also elemental that we experience the day and enjoy the weather. Seeing the sky, feeling the mist of a light rain on your face, taking a short but invigorating walk around the block—these things can refresh us more deeply than a cup of caffeine or a trip to the vending machine.

Before there were coffee breaks, long lunches, and aspirin, there was the sun, the sky, and the air. Take pleasure in them and enjoy the voluptuous peace that results. Outdoor recess is not only for children.

TODAY'S LESSON:

I will go outside and experience the day.

PEACE

True happiness depends on a quiet soul.

—GEORGE WASHINGTON

Some times the reason why our class is a terror is that we're terrified inside. Often the classroom is a mirror. They say the character defects you abhor in others are the ones you have yourself.

We may be unhappy with our teaching assignments, coworkers, or students because our own souls are agitated. How can we still our own souls? Some gentle questioning may be in order. Perhaps instead of being in the teacher mode, we need to take on an attitude of learning. Perhaps we need a break from routine. It could be that we need to throw ourselves more fully into the task at hand. Allowing space and time to be quiet will help reveal the next step that will move us closer to serenity and harmony.

TODAY'S LESSON:
I reflect on those things that give me peace.

SERVICE

Kindness is the best remedy for suffering.

—MOZAMBIQUE PROVERB

Because to be a child is often synonymous with being vulnerable, we are sensitive to the needs and feelings of the young people in our charge. We are patient with the immigrant boy who speaks halting English. We take pains to draw out the girl in the third row, giving her an important task to handle in order to nurture her fledgling leadership skills.

But children are not the only ones who need our listening ear or gentle touch. The teacher down the hall is going through a divorce. The secretary is facing surgery next week. The custodian's son was arrested yesterday and you can see the worry that has etched itself on his face overnight.

We may dismiss the problems of other adults who are not our buddies by saying, "That's life" or "I've got problems of my own to cope with." You don't have to become the faculty therapist, but that doesn't mean you aren't a point of healing in your circle of contacts. True, you aren't being paid to help. Yet isn't helping the real reason you're here?

TODAY'S LESSON:
I am my brother's or sister's keeper.

PURPOSE

To love what you do and feel that it matters—how could anything be more fun?

—KATHARINE GRAHAM

Teachers have something that many factory workers, used car salesmen, chairmen of the board, executive secretaries, and tax attorneys don't have. The work that teachers do can be life-changing. We are not turning out widgets, trying to please wealthy stockholders, or finagling a deal for greedy lawyers. Something said or done in our class can leave a mark that lasts for decades.

There is no law that compels you to go to church or temple to hear an inspired message. There's no assurance that you'll meet and marry your soul mate and be transformed forever by love. But there is a law that says all young people must attend school and that there will be a teacher there waiting to teach them. That teacher is you.

Whether we've wanted to teach all our lives or just happened into the job—now that we're here we have the power and the glory to touch someone's life.

TODAY'S LESSON:

It is an honor to teach.

FLEXIBILITY

Every successful enterprise requires three men—
a dreamer, a businessman, and a son of a bitch.

—PETER MCARTHUR

Running a good class is like playing every position in a football game. A teacher has to be like a quarterback who masterminds the action; a coach who mentors and motivates the team; a referee who enforces the rules (and occasionally breaks up fights); an announcer who gives a play-by-play progress report for the public and the front office; and a cheerleader who encourages everyone to do their best.

TODAY'S LESSON:

I strive for versatility.

JOY

Why torture yourself when life will do it for you?

—LAURA WALKER

Sometimes we take the world too seriously. We're here to have fun, as much as we're here to work, or to learn, or to serve. In fact, if there's no enjoyment in working, learning, or serving, that pretty much nullifies any of the good that comes from doing those things. If all of our attention is taken up with obligations and anxieties, it can add up to a dreary daily existence. Given that reality, don't leave fun out of the equation.

Life presents enough issues that will cause stress, strain, and pain. The least we can do—and the best we can do—is to walk our paths with as much joy as we can stand.

TODAY'S LESSON:
Having fun is on the day's agenda.

LOVE

The love of flowers is really the best teacher of how to grow and understand.

—MAX SCHLING

Love is the starting point, the initiating incident for anything that's going to be glorious, good, or successful. Let something or someone you love make your effort worthwhile: love of children; love of Spanish or statistics or science or whatever the subject you teach; love of education; or even the love you have for your own family, which pushes you out of bed and propels you out the door each morning to come to work so that you earn money enough to support them. Love makes you do things you would ordinarily refuse to do. It will make you arrive early, stay late, miss lunch, try harder.

45

If you are not led by love, you will be driven by something else. Why let selfishness, laziness, or anxiety rule your actions? Let love rule and be free.

TODAY'S LESSON:
My actions originate from a base of love.

SERVICE

*The best of leaders are those when the job is done, when the task is accomplished,
the people will say, "We have done it ourselves."*

—LAO-TSU

One weekend while watching a 1930s movie, I thrilled at the sight of Fred Astaire and Ginger Rogers dancing. In this particular number, Fred mostly glided around looking debonair, while Ginger was turning and spinning like a whirlwind, being tossed high in the air and having to land gracefully and on beat. In other words, she was doing all the work while Fred was basically standing there and looking good. I thought of her statement—"I did everything Fred Astaire did, except backwards and in high heels." Her part of the partnership was the more intricate and more demanding, yet *he* was the one who got top billing and higher pay.

Teaching often requires selfless giving (as does being married or being a parent). We work hard, real hard. We plan, we implement, we execute. We do a lot of the groundbreaking and foundation-making, executing the tasks that are often not visible once the job is done. Effective teachers must do a lot behind the scenes so that the students can be the stars on stage.

TODAY'S LESSON:

Sometimes I am willing to work backstage
in order for my students to shine.

GRATITUDE

When you are kind to someone in trouble, you hope they'll remember and be kind to someone else. And it'll become like a wildfire.

—WHOOPI GOLDBERG

There are two ways to say "thanks." One way is to say it or show it to the person who did you the favor. The other way is to demonstrate your appreciation by doing a kindness to someone else.

If you really want to be advanced, do both.

TODAY'S LESSON:

I can do someone a good turn.

ORGANIZATION

*Children have never been good at listening to their elders,
but they have never failed to imitate them.*

—JAMES BALDWIN

It seems obvious, but my students did the best work and were the most productive when I was the most organized. When I presented lessons that challenged students' thinking and creativity, they responded with enthusiasm, even though these lessons demanded more work from them and from me to develop. When I showed up for class adequately rested and ready to work on my part, it triggered an attitude of serenity and a willingness to get down to business on their part. A well-thought-out lesson, rules that are clear—these add up to an atmosphere that is conducive to learning.

Would your teaching practice benefit from the addition of more structure?

TODAY'S LESSON:

I go the extra mile to prepare for class.

ENDURANCE

But those who wait on the Lord shall renew their strength, they shall mount up with wings like eagles, they shall run and not be weary, they shall walk and not faint.

—ISAIAH 40:31

You would think that as you make progress in life, you would be able to soar through life rather than plod through it. But the progression reflected in this verse suggests just the opposite—first you fly, then you run, finally, you walk. Walking is slow. Walking is plain and ordinary. Walking is unimpressive.

Flying is high technology. To get and keep a plane aloft you need a team of experts. Running is swift, but it will wear you out. Running makes your heart race and your feet sore and if you're not careful, it will put you out of commission fast.

But steady walking is what can carry you through the long haul. Walking allows you to take in the sights. Walking allows you to smell the flowers. Maybe even pause and plant a flower or two.

Walking is something you do every day. And that is what a good life is like—a daily walk. A journey where you thoughtfully observe what is around you, enjoy the path you're on, stop to plant a seed in someone's life that, hopefully, will produce fruit long after you are gone. We are all sojourners, learning to walk the walk and not just talk the talk. Now *that's* impressive.

TODAY'S LESSON:

Steady growth is healthy growth.

COURAGE

You lose a wallet or keys or something and you notice in a second.
But your life can go missing and you don't even know it.

—JOHN DUFRESNE

I attended a workshop on counseling people who have HIV or AIDS. As the workshop leader discussed the mental health issues concerning this serious illness, he made the remark, "Of course, there are several good things that come out of having AIDS."

"Excuse me," I had to interrupt. "Exactly what could be good about having AIDS?"

"Well, first of all, once you realize you have AIDS," the counselor explained, "you know that if there's anything you've ever wanted to do, you'd better do it. If there's anybody you need to forgive, you forgive them. If there's anything you need to correct, you change it. Those things alone cause some people to live a much better life than they had been up to that point."

Taken in that light, a dread disease could be a blessing. But why wait till the doctor approaches us with bad news? We already know that our time here is limited. We know that giving and forgiving are more gratifying than grasping and grudge-bearing. Given that knowledge, it is time to act.

TODAY'S LESSON:

I have the courage to live.

FOCUS

I spend all my time living in the now, *not in the* way back when
or the one day when.

—JOAN RIVERS

Maybe next semester they won't place all the behavior problems in your class. You dream about the day you get a class of obedient pupils. Maybe the best principal you ever worked for was the one you had five years ago. If only she would come back to your school. What if the school board ever decided to pay teachers what they're really worth? What I could do with that money!

These kinds of thoughts are pleasant enough for a visit—but you don't want to make a home living in the fantasy world of maybe, what if, and if only. Too much time spent "back in the day" prevents you from maximizing the here and now. Now is a good place to be. Now is where life is taking place. Now is where the beginning of good changes starts. Now is when you enjoy the fruits of what was started yesterday.

The good old days were once now. Did you appreciate the good old days when they were nowadays? Today was once the rosy future you were looking forward to. Now that the future is here, are you able to enjoy it?

Yes, enjoy pleasant memories from the past. And yes, make good plans for the future. And yes, most emphatically, say yes to the now.

TODAY'S LESSON:

I live in the present.

VITALITY

You have to live life to love life, and you have to love life to live life. It's a vicious circle.

—ANONYMOUS

I know I'm guilty of thinking, *If I can just last till dismissal time* or *If only June would hurry up and get here.* Too often, I'm focused on when the day, the year, the moment will be over—*then* I'll be satisfied. When I'm retired, *then* I'll be happy. The truth is, when we're retired, we will probably miss the hustle-bustle, color, and clamor of the activities that are driving us crazy now. While this moment is here, we get to experience the wonderful, the weird, and the wearying—the levity and the gravity of working and talking and striving with others. These moments are not the fringes but the fabric of existence, not the edges but the very essence of life. Don't kill time, thinking you are saving something for later. Don't kill time; time is what your life is made of. The point of life is not to get to the end of it, but to live it fully, all the way to the end.

TODAY'S LESSON:

I cherish both the good and trying parts of my job.

TRANQUILITY

The devil is easy to identify. He appears when you're terribly tired and makes a very reasonable request which you know you shouldn't grant.

—FIORELLO LA GUARDIA

Lesson plans. Grading papers. PTA. Revising curriculum. Faculty meetings. And now the principal wants me to fill out still another meaningless complicated form and have it on his desk by close of business. Plus, I never did finish the report the department head requires. And once I get out of here, exactly what will I cook for dinner?

Slow down.

Are you feeling harried, hustled? That you can't balance one more thing? Like you don't need another task to do? You're probably right.

Slow down.

Breathe deeply. Not everything that needs to be done needs to be done right now. Not every decision that needs to be made needs to be made right now. Maybe you need to say no.

TODAY'S LESSON:

I will think about all the things I'm asked to do today and decide to which I need to say yes, to which I need to say no, and to which I need to say later.

CHANGE

Education's purpose is to replace an empty mind with an open one.

—MALCOLM S. FORBES

Okay. You've slowed down. You've stopped running so fast. Your thoughts have quit racing. Your mind is now empty. So what do you do now? What's supposed to happen next?

It's not that your mind is supposed to remain a sieve, full of nothing. We clear our minds of the old thoughts and ideas so that the new thoughts can have a clean residence. A bowl that's full of dirt has to be emptied and cleaned before it can be filled with water to drink. We set aside the previous information so that the updated information has a place to be. When this is done, we have extended an invitation not only to new information but possibly to transformation.

TODAY'S LESSON:

I'm open to possibilities.

FLEXIBILITY

My job is to be resilient. That's why I call life a dance.

—BILL T. JONES

It takes wisdom to be able to know when to hold the line versus when to loosen one's grip. Will the bad boy respond best to a tough love approach? Or is he acting out because he longs for more compassion in his life, not more rules and restrictions? Is the department chair someone who will get off my back if I show her I don't take any guff, or will my hard stance harden her against me?

Life's sticky situations can't be solved with a one-size-fits-all multipurpose elixir. If one-size-fits-all is a lie for panty hose, you know it doesn't work in real life. So what does work? Staying open and remaining flexible.

TODAY'S LESSON:

I make adjustments to fit the occasion.

UNITY

There is no us and them, there is only us.

—BILL CLINTON

Students vs. teachers. Teachers vs. administrators. School vs. community. Opposites don't have to be opposing forces. Opposites can be thought of as two aspects of the same thing. After all, it's not possible to have a coin with a front but no back, a box with an inside but no outside—or a school without teachers and students, parents and principals.

When we think of people who are different from us as complements, then we no longer have to treat them as foes. Instead, we can see ourselves as parts of a cooperative pair, each offering a distinct but necessary perspective.

So what if someone's philosophy is left wing and someone else's is right wing? No bird, nor any aircraft, flies with only one wing. Wings on each side are needed for anything to fly.

Wouldn't it be a relief to realize that any opponent is ultimately on our side? If you could believe that, how would you treat the other person?

TODAY'S LESSON:

I treat others with respect.

HONESTY

Man was made for Joy and Woe / And when this we rightly know /
Through the World we safely go.

—WILLIAM BLAKE

There's a philosophy that states that all "negative" feelings should be avoided and neutralized. If you're feeling guilty, depressed, angry, or saddened you should "think positive" and change your attitude. But being positive is only one half of the situation, and you need two halves to make one whole. Negative is not necessarily synonymous with bad. If you feel guilty, it may well be because you've done something wrong. If you're down on your luck, or you've sustained a loss, it's healthy to be sad or depressed. Has someone violated you? Anger is a normal reaction.

These feelings exist for a reason. They are real. Plastering over these emotions doesn't make them go away. They just burrow deeper inside, then burst out at a later (and usually a far more inconvenient) time and place when they refuse to be denied.

It is far better to feel the feeling and make an appropriate response than to pretend the emotion and its message don't exist.

If we are feeling guilty because we've wronged someone, then we apologize and make restitution. If we are feeling sad and down, we may need to take time to grieve, reflect, and be gentle with our souls. If we're angry, we may need to let the offender know his or her behavior is out of order so that the person may have the chance to correct it.

TODAY'S LESSON:

I am honest with myself about what I'm feeling.

ACTION

Words are a form of action, capable of influencing change.

—INGRID BENGIS

Talk is cheap . . . well, yes—if you're substituting talk for action. But when talking represents momentum and progress into a new direction, then talk *is* action.

This type of action-oriented conversation is likely to be the kind that gives voice to the issue that's on everyone's mind but no one heretofore has had the courage to express. This type of talk is a discussion where differences are put on the table and sorted out. This is the type of talk for meeting eye to eye, going toe-to-toe and touching heart to heart. This is not chitchat or small talk. This kind of talk hits at the gut level.

When talk addresses the matters that are vital and weighty and the talkers are vigorously honest, events have no choice but to change.

TODAY'S LESSON:

I am forthright in my speech.

ACHIEVEMENT

*We must concentrate on what we can do and erase "can't," "won't,"
and "don't think so" from our vocabulary.*

—CARDISS COLLINS

You have too many four-letter words in your vocabulary. Here are the
ones you need to eliminate first:

can't
won't
don't
hate
fear
lazy
hard luck

TODAY'S LESSON:

I take a positive attitude.

GROWTH

After the verb "to love," "to help" is the most beautiful verb in the world.

—BERTHA VON SUTTNER

You need more four-letter words in your vocabulary. Here are a few to help you get started:

> hope
> help
> sing
> feel
> grow
> pray
> play
> make love
> live life

TODAY'S LESSON:

I act on the positive.

INTEGRITY

It's best to let our titles define what we do and let God define who we are.

—BARBARA REYNOLDS

To profess something is to make a statement or affirmation. It is to bear witness to the truth of a matter. Profess was once a religious term. A clergyman would wait to discern his call, and then once it was clear, he would state or *profess* what he was to do: In other words, state his profession. Is your profession a statement of who you are? Is the way you do your job, your profession, a reflection of integrity? Can others bear witness to the fact that you are whom you profess yourself to be?

If you cannot give proactive responses to these questions, then what can you do to line up your practice with your philosophy?

We may not be working in the educational field because we feel a divine imperative to do so. But while we are employed in this position we can do a worthy job. We can act with integrity. "Practice what you preach" applies to both preachers and teachers.

TODAY'S LESSON:

My actions and my words are in alignment.

INSTRUCTION

We learn to do something by doing it. There is no other way.

—JOHN HOLT

Reading a book about swimming is nothing like swimming. It's not even close. You can't learn how to float by attending a lecture on it. Doing is believing, doing is learning, doing is knowing.

Sometimes our lessons lack a "hands-on" component. It's all listen-to-the-lecture or look-at-the-book. Are there manipulatives we can use to introduce a concept? Would a field trip enhance the class? Is there some way we can incorporate art or music to make the lesson more stimulating?

You learned how to do most of the fun things you do by *doing* them, not by sitting in a classroom—dancing, singing, playing cards, playing tennis, taking pictures, lovemaking. You learned how to do many of the practical things you do by *doing* them, not by reading a book—cooking, driving, cleaning, or fixing things around the house, grocery shopping, budgeting . . . even teaching.

Our students will learn best in the same way.

TODAY'S LESSON:

I can include an experiential aspect to my instruction.

PATIENCE

Sometimes when I look at my children, I say to myself, Lillian, you should have stayed a virgin.

—LILLIAN CARTER

Some days when you look at the children in your class, you think—I should have become a plumber. Children can be cruel, devious, exasperating, treacherous. At least when adults behave like beasts, you can curse them out, tell them to get lost, or sue them in court.

But when Johnny tries your nerves, the most you can do is tell his mama, who may not be able to control the little darling, either. People who don't work in a school sometimes naïvely think that the main thing teachers do all day is play with children. Ha. Children are not all sweetness and light, charm and charisma. It takes tough love, long suffering, and the ability to laugh at it all.

TODAY'S LESSON:

I must keep my perspective.

REST

If it hadn't been for June, July, and August, I would have committed suicide.

—RETIRED TEACHER

What do picking cotton, working on a chain gang, and teaching have in common? They're tough work. Teaching is love- and labor-intensive, emotionally exacting and exhausting. We give big, which means we have to dig deep to replenish ourselves. Don't wait till spring break or summer vacation to catch a breather. You need rest on a daily basis.

Make sure you get it.

TODAY'S LESSON:
I make time to rest properly.

ADVERSITY

I merely took the energy it takes to pout and wrote some blues.

—DUKE ELLINGTON

Carolina Maria de Jesus, a black Brazilian mother, was born in abject poverty in a shantytown near São Paulo. She fed herself and her three children by foraging in garbage. To keep from dwelling on her misery, she would write. She explains what writing did for her soul: ". . . when I was writing, I was in a golden palace, with crystal windows and silver chandeliers. My dress was finest satin and diamonds sat shining in my black hair. Then I put away my book and the smells came in through the rotting walls and rats ran over my feet. My satin turned to rags and the only things shining in my hair were lice."

She ended up writing a diary about slum life entitled *Beyond All Pity.* It was published in 1960 and sold ten thousand copies in three days. It stayed on the best-seller list for two years and at that time sold more copies than any other Brazilian book ever had.

Carolina Maria de Jesus had a second-grade education.

TODAY'S LESSON:

My imagination can save my soul.

GROWTH

Insanity is doing the same thing over and over again, but expecting different results.

—ALCOHOLICS ANONYMOUS

No matter what school you're assigned to, do you always end up working for a crazy, crabby principal? Do you constantly find the student who grates on your nerves showing up in your room, year after year? "This time will be different" you told yourself when you remarried, only to discover the sad truth that your new spouse is abnormal in the same exasperating ways as the last one.

When you find yourself repeating the same pattern over and over again, the universe is trying to give you a message. There's something in the way you handle (or fail to handle) these situations that needs to change. Once you've learned your lesson and made the change in behavior or attitude, you'll find that the external situation almost always improves. Otherwise, if you keep doing what you're doing, you'll keep getting what you're getting

Are you ready to change?

TODAY'S LESSON:

I am ready to change.

TRANQUILITY

All you need to do to receive guidance is to ask for it and then listen.

—SANAYA ROMAN

Where do good ideas come from? How do they originate? Many good ideas slip in when you're unawares. They come when the mind is relaxed or distracted, when driving the car or walking the dog.

If we fill up our day with too much activity and busy-ness, we won't have many good ideas. We will have crowded them out. It's almost easier to talk on the phone, handle a hundred papers, run myriad errands, stay perpetually in motion than to be still.

However, when we make room for stillness, the return on the investment is rewarding.

TODAY'S LESSON:

I sit still long enough to receive the good idea that is now forming.

PERSEVERANCE

You may be disappointed if you fail, but you are doomed if you don't try.

—BEVERLY SILLS

The child who never masters reading will be handicapped by his weak literacy skills all of his life, but he doesn't believe you when you say it's important. "What does this have to do with anything?" he complains. "Why do I have to learn this?"

Some of the lessons life is trying to teach us fall under the same category. Rebuilding a relationship. Sticking to a diet. Completing a course of study. There are no guarantees of success if we work at it; only the assurance of failure if we do not.

TODAY'S LESSON:

I commit to completing what I have started.

APPRECIATION

Magical power, marvelous action, chop wood, carry water.

—CHINESE ZEN MASTER

The regular routine. The same-old same-old. The daily grind. Every day we get up to "meet the mule" as the folks down home used to say. There is much about work that is uneventful. And much about teaching that does not change from day to day or year to year. This is not a bad thing. The regular routine is what you will miss when the unexpected shift occurs. The same-old same-old is what gives comfort and familiarity to our day. It doesn't have to be a daily grind, however. When we have mastered the nuts and bolts of our job and it has become second nature, we can embellish the basics. Then we can experiment, take risks, wander away from the norm, knowing that we know the way back home. Work then becomes play. What's the difference between work and play? Play is work you enjoy.

TODAY'S LESSON:

The ordinary is perfection.

LOVE

Love is the magician, the enchanter, that changes worthless things to joy,
and makes right royal kings and queens of common clay.

—ROBERT G. INGERSOLL

Overheard at a retirement dinner:

" I'll miss Coach. He deserves the award he's getting tonight."

"He sure does, although when he talked he couldn't ever make his subject and verb agree."

"But he sure could get the boys on the football team to play their hearts out."

"Why did all the kids like Coach? It must be because sports are always the most popular part of any high school."

"That couldn't have been the whole story. He wasn't exactly the sharpest knife in the drawer . . . I think one or two footballs hit him in the head. Yet, he was still able to take the team to the playoffs every year."

"True. He'd always say, '*Boy, do I love these kids . . .*'

TODAY'S LESSON:

I love my students.

INSTRUCTION

The grass may be greener on the other side but it's just as hard to cut.

—LITTLE RICHARD

There are two types of instructor. One is a traffic cop. The traffic cop tells pupils when to start and when to stop. He or she points the direction in which they are to proceed, without taking the trip along with the student. The cop is a respected authority figure. The other type is a choreographer. The choreographer demonstrates the moves, then watches to see the student execute it. He or she doesn't only tell what to do but shows how to do it. The dancer is making a work of art. The police officer is establishing a clear path to help people move freely to their destinations.

Our personal style may place us in one camp or the other. We may wish we could loosen up and be as "limber" as the choreographer, or wish we could command the respect that the police officer wields. Whether we are cops or choreographers, there are strengths and weaknesses to either approach. The best thing to do is to adapt what we can from the other approach as well as honor our own.

TODAY'S LESSON:

I respect my style even as I learn from others.

GROWTH

The real fault is to have faults and not to amend them.

—CONFUCIUS

The way to escape being a loser is to be a chooser. Choose to get back up when you're knocked down. Choose to work sharper, when you're too bushed to work harder. Choose a different road when you face a detour.

Every man, woman, and child ends up on the short end of the stick from time to time. And when that happens, every man, woman, and child has the option of making a new choice. They may choose to make that stick a club with which they beat themselves up. Or they can use it as the staff to lean on as they move forward.

TODAY'S LESSON:

I choose to work on my shortcomings.

72

INSIGHT

We suffer primarily not from our vices or our weaknesses, but from our illusions. We are haunted, not by reality, but by those images we have put in place of reality.

—DANIEL J. BOORSTIN

Prince Charming had a flat tire on the way to your house, so he won't be coming. Your ship is not coming in, either. The secret formula remains a secret. And you don't have the winning lottery ticket.

This is good news. When you are freed from living in fantasies, you get to work with what *is*, not with illusion. The first word in illusion is "ill." Facing reality may not be fun, but it is healthy. There's really no alternative to being here, living now, and existing in the real world. If you're not *now here*, then you're *nowhere*.

TODAY'S LESSON:

I accept what is real.

ADVERSITY

We must embrace pain and burn it as fuel for our journey.

—KENJI MIYAZAWA

After years of working at it, praying for it, and hoping against hope, a woman's marriage came to an end anyway. The devastation of the end of the relationship left her in mourning. Every romantic song on the radio made her weepy, every memory left her depressed. She began looking for ways to escape thinking about it. "Don't do that," a friend told her. "You may as well grieve over it now."

"Why should I when I can act as if it didn't happen and not have to feel these feelings?"

"Because the grief won't really go away just because you pretend it isn't there," her friend replied. "It'll just go underground and find the weakest part of your body and attack you there. Next thing you know, you're grieving *and* sick."

The paradox is that in accepting pain you ultimately suffer less pain than if you attempt to avoid it. The challenge is to take the pain and make it productive. Allow it to become the catalyst for a comeback, the hurt that makes you more sensitive, the experience that strengthens character, the power that transports you to a stronger place.

TODAY'S LESSON:

I have courage.

GOAL SETTING

We judge ourselves by what we feel capable of doing,
but others judge us by what we have already done.

—LEO TOLSTOY

What were you doing last year this time? If you were questioned then about how you would like to change your life in the coming twelve months, what would you have said? Have those goals become realities? Maybe you hope to lose weight, get more education, improve relations with someone at home, save some money.

None of those things will happen if you keep putting them off. Name your goals. Write them down. Now, do at least one small thing that will put you on the road to seeing your dreams become fact.

TODAY'S LESSON:

Now is the time.

ENCOURAGEMENT

Every blade of grass has its angel that bends over it and whispers, "Grow, grow."

—THE TALMUD

The yew tree grows in the Pacific Northwest region of the United States. At one time it was in danger of extinction, but that was not much of a concern since it was believed that the yew tree did not have any particular usefulness. It got in the way of the harvesting of other trees that were prized for lumber and therefore was destroyed with no thought of replanting.

However, it was discovered that the bark of the yew tree was useful in the treatment of cancer. All of a sudden, the yew tree became important, too.

There is a yew tree growing in your classroom.

TODAY'S LESSON:

I value every student in my class.

INSTRUCTION

Overture! Curtain, lights. This is it, to hit the heights. And o, what heights we'll hit.
On with the show—this is it!

—"BUGS BUNNY" THEME SONG

What was your favorite TV cartoon as a kid? Can you sing the theme music to that show? I'm willing to bet you can. I know all the words to the Bugs Bunny overture although I never sat down and consciously tried to memorize it. But the repetition, the catchy music, and my own enjoyment of the program left an imprint on my mind such that I learned it without ever trying to. Would that all teaching and learning could be so easy.

Well, we can take some of what works in popular culture and bring it into the classroom. Some people learn more easily when music or rhythm is added. Bringing in objects for students to manipulate helps concepts become more concrete. Not everyone learns by a strictly academic approach. The learning curve increases when an instructor can respond to the different learning styles of the students.

TODAY'S LESSON:

I incorporate varied approaches in my teaching style.

DISCIPLINE

A sequential chain of events called growth will bring forth the fruits of the seeds.

—REVEREND JOE HILL

Millions of Americans are overweight. Is it because obesity is like cancer—a disease for which there is no cure? Are people confused about what the remedy could be? To the contrary, everyone knows what is required to lose weight. Eat less and exercise more. The problem is not a lack of knowledge but an unwillingness to do the work.

The reason that some teachers don't improve is that we aren't willing to do the necessary work. We groan at the thought of reworking the curriculum. We find an excuse to miss the upcoming in-service. We never ask other teachers what works in their classrooms. We are not curious to read the new literature.

It takes an effort to nudge ourselves out of the familiar routine and take on a harder task. It takes an effort, but it may not take a major effort. We can take baby steps to effect change—agreeing to vary our routine just a bit or deciding to have an open mind when attending the staff development program. Becoming willing to become more willing is the hinge that will open the door.

TODAY'S LESSON:

I am willing to take steps in a new direction.

GOAL SETTING

Action is the antidote to despair.

—JOAN BAEZ

How would you like to become known for being an incompetent worker? What about gaining weight until your health is in jeopardy? How would you like to be so far in debt that you begin to consider committing a crime to get money? What about losing out on an increase in pay because you never made it back to school?

These are not things we plan to happen or ever want to happen. These are not the goals we set for ourselves. But these things sometimes happen precisely because we have failed to set goals or make plans. We get too caught up in the busy-ness of life to take care of business . . . to take care of our lives.

79

TODAY'S LESSON:

I will write down three things I'd like to achieve
and a timetable for achieving them.

BOUNDARIES

Saying "no" can be the ultimate in self care.

—CLAUDIA BLACK

"Why don't you take on the graduation this year?"

"I know you won't mind if I use your supplies, right?"

"Could you pick up something for me on your way home from work?"

It's a tricky business; discerning when saying no is being selfish and when saying no is wisdom. When guilt, fatigue, and a desperate need to please are motivating us, that may be an indication that saying yes is the wrong answer. Being able to say no keeps us from taking detours from the path we're supposed to be on. It prevents us from having regrets farther down the road. Instead of being an act of selfishness, sometimes saying no is an act of self-preservation.

TODAY'S LESSON:

Saying no can bring peace of mind.

CHANGE

I change myself, I change the world.

—GLORIA ANZALDÚA

How do you—
Change your mind—open it.
Change your position—move it.
Change your routine—break it.
Change your fortune—risk it.
Change your attitude—improve it.
Change your community—lead it.
Change your world—love it.

TODAY'S LESSON:

I'm not afraid to try something new.

KNOWLEDGE

Everyone is an idiot, not just the people with low SAT scores. The only difference among us is that we're idiots about different things at different times.

—SCOTT ADAMS

In the tenth grade, I entered a suburban high school that had an outstanding academic reputation. Prior to that, I had attended public schools in the city and although I was a good student, I was very much aware that at my new school, the students were supposed to be very smart.

As a teen in the city, I was used to catching the bus to get around town. If I wanted to go downtown to shop, visit a girlfriend, or see a movie, I asked my mother for permission to go—and then I was gone. To my amazement, I found the situation a lot different for my suburban friends. Many of them never rode the bus and, to go anywhere, had to wait for their mom or dad to chauffeur them, or had to cajole them for the car keys. Moreover, not only were they unfamiliar with the bus, but they were afraid to ride it—afraid of getting lost, apprehensive about learning how to navigate on public transportation, unused to walking short distances.

This experience showed me that even if I lacked some formal knowledge, I possessed valuable practical knowledge that the suburban students lacked and were the lesser for. I didn't have to feel diminished or intimidated in my new academic environment, for just as they knew things I did not know, I knew that I knew some things—important and useful things—that they did not know.

TODAY'S LESSON:

I respect different forms of intelligence.

AGING

I don't want to achieve immortality by being inducted into baseball's Hall of Fame. I want to achieve immortality by not dying.

—LEO DUROCHER

There's no alternative to old age. Well, actually there is one alternative, but most of us want to put that off for as many years as we can, which means we would like to live a long time. And that means we will get old.

Aging is a natural part of the process of life as is youth. It has its charms as does childhood, it is as precious as is infancy. Whether we are growing up or growing old, the important idea is to grow.

TODAY'S LESSON:
I accept my age.

RECIPROCITY

How far you go in life depends on your being tender with the young, compassionate with the aged, sympathetic with the striving, and tolerant of the weak and the strong, because someday in life you will have been all of these.

—GEORGE WASHINGTON CARVER

I've been told that everybody is the forty-second cousin of everyone else on the planet. That means we are all related. And if we're all connected, each of us has an influence on each other. That means the way you treat the girl in the back row, the comments you make about the superintendent, the greeting you gave to the school secretary, the attitude you have toward the parents of the boy you asked to be suspended all affect you.

Keeping that in mind, we are conscious of how we interact with others. That does not mean we have to act like a Pollyanna around people who should be corrected, avoided, or ignored. That sort of false positive behavior is dishonest . . . sometimes dangerous. Rather, we treat others the way we want to be treated, in full knowledge that eventually whatever we send out will come back to us.

TODAY'S LESSON:

I get back what I give.

ACTION

Better to try all things and to find all empty,
than to try nothing and leave your life a blank.

—CHARLOTTE BRONTË

Grad school seemed like an idea worth considering. There was a program at a nearby university and Derry was thinking about enrolling. The only problem was that with a full-time teaching job and a family to support, Derry would only be able to attend school part time. That meant a two-year degree could take five years to complete.

"Not worth it," he concluded.

"Not worth it?" a colleague questioned him when he announced his decision. "Won't you qualify for a raise once you get another degree?"

"That's true," Derry conceded, "but it'll take so long to get the degree. Five years is a long time to wait."

"Five years is going to pass whether you go to school or not," countered the other teacher. "You might as well go ahead and do it so that five years from now you'll have the raise and the degree rather than have nothing."

TODAY'S LESSON:

Tomorrow's big achievements begin with today's small actions.

DISCIPLINE

Good fellows are a dime a dozen, but an aggressive leader is priceless.

—EARL "RED" BLAIR

My very first day working at a school was as the substitute teacher for a fourth grade. I stood at the door to greet students as they arrived and noticed the teacher of the class next door. Her students lined up in a straight row, didn't chatter, didn't budge, didn't peep. One boy made the mistake of wiggling while he was walking into the room and she snapped, "Okay, Thomas—you just lost your privilege for recess."

"Man, she's mean," I thought. "I'm not going to be that harsh." I closed the door and went into my room, where the students all decided to have a day-long indoor recess. I was trying to be liked rather than establishing myself as the authority and, boy, did those children take advantage of my naïveté. I began to wish I could get some quick lessons in being "mean" from the teacher next door. Although at that point, I no longer regarded her as being mean, but as knowing how to discipline. Without classroom management skills, no class can take place.

TODAY'S LESSON:

I establish and maintain discipline in my room.

HUMILITY

Struggle to learn, learn to struggle.

—FRANK BONILLA

I was leading a creative writing club for middle school students. These children loved to write and took themselves seriously. Their teachers, their parents, and their classmates had all told them they were good at their craft. Some of them had won awards or had poems published. Whenever I assigned an exercise, they always completed it. If I said write a poem, they'd write a poem. If I said write ten poems, they wrote ten poems.

But I was intimidated by these preteens. As a writer myself, I frequently had a hard time disciplining myself to write and produce consistently. I was humbled by my students' obedience to their craft. Their example helped me modify my own behavior. Their discipline shamed me into becoming more disciplined. I became my students' student.

TODAY'S LESSON:

I have as much to learn as I have to teach.

INTEGRITY

To be who you are and become what you are capable of is the only goal worth living.

—ALVIN AILEY

When we hear someone described as a "Romeo," we know he is a sexy or romantic man. When we hear the word "Einstein," we think genius, brains, and intelligence. If someone is described as another Mother Teresa we imagine that person to possess great compassion and love.

What qualities do people associate with your name? Do they associate you with the virtues you aspire to have? Is your name synonymous with effective teacher? Supportive friend? Sharp thinker? Good listener?

If not, what can you do to improve your game in order to match your name with your fame?

TODAY'S LESSON:

My walk matches my talk.

FRIENDSHIP

I desire you would open and clear your eyes.

—TEEDYUSCUNG

Antelopes are graceful animals. They can run fast, smell keenly, and hear well. Their vision is not as well developed. It is said that antelopes walk side by side so that they can blow the sand from each other's eyes.

A good friend is like an antelope.

TODAY'S LESSON:

I am of service to my friends.

HEALTH

If you don't take care of your body, where will you live?

—ANONYMOUS

An Olympic runner. A soccer player. A chorus line dancer. A construction worker. A longshoreman. These are occupations where it's obvious that physical health and stamina are critical. The same is true of teaching. Good physical condition is instrumental to one's ability to do any job because with any job, the primary instrument used is the body. When we have respected our instrument through regular exercise, healthy eating habits, and drinking lots of water, we have more stamina for pursuits in and outside the school. We think better, perform better, and feel better, too.

TODAY'S LESSON:

I take care of my body.

FEAR

The death of fear is in doing what we fear to do.

—NATIVE AMERICAN PROVERB

I once heard a woman say that the two things she feared most were getting fat and getting old. "Since I am both overweight and over forty, then I must be fearless!" she declared. Trying not to think about our fears, trying to avoid situations that will put us face to face with the things that make us uneasy, or pretending they don't exist never works forever. What are you afraid of? What are you going to do about it?

TODAY'S LESSON:

I identify one thing I fear and ask for help to overcome it.

UNITY

A single twig breaks, but the bundle of twigs is strong.

—SHAWNEE CHIEF BLUE JACKET

Maybe the thing you're attempting to do is failing because you're doing it alone. Most folks do not like to ask for help. Nobody likes to fail, either. When your desire to succeed supersedes your pride, help arrives and triumph follows.

Asking for help does not diminish the asker. It is a sign of clarity and strength to recognize your need of others. When joined together, we boost the odds for victory and even should we fail, togetherness buffers the defeat. Either way we win, if we unite.

TODAY'S LESSON:

I am willing to ask for and receive help.

INTEGRITY

A man who does not benefit the world by his life does it by his death.

—NINETEENTH-CENTURY SAYING

What will be written in your obituary?

What will people whisper about you at the funeral? Will they describe you as a good teacher? Or someone who was just showing up to collect a check? A good listener, there in times of crisis? Or a self-absorbed busybody, too selfishly preoccupied to give anyone else a moment's thought?

How will your students remember you? As the adult who inspired them, taught them the information that has now made them productive citizens? Or the mean and petty instructor who bored them silly, punished unfairly, graded too hard.

Those who have had near-death experiences report that just before the end, their whole life flashed before their eyes like a movie. When that moment comes for you, will what you see be a satisfying action adventure, a love story, or a tragedy?

TODAY'S LESSON:

I am working on my character flaws.

ADVERSITY

Our own healing proceeds from that overlap of what we call good and evil, light and dark. It is not the light element alone does the healing; the place where light and dark begin to touch is where miracles arise.

—ROBERT A. JOHNSON

When we are troubled, we often call that time a period of darkness, a dark night of the soul.

Darkness is a good thing.

It's during the hushed hours of the night you think serious thoughts. Rest, sleep, and dreams are events that take place when the lights go out and the sun goes down. When praying, we often close our eyes to shut out daylight in order for a deeper illumination to reveal itself.

The period of darkness you're enduring is the incubator for the recovery that is next to emerge.

TODAY'S LESSON:

I am patient.

AWARENESS

Education is when you read the fine print. Experience is what you get if you don't.

—PETE SEEGER

One's intuition is almost always ahead of the intellect. Words say anything but behavior doesn't lie if you know how to read it. *I should have known* we say to ourselves when the funny feeling, the persistent thought, or the warning signal that we pooh-poohed turns out to have been dead on the money. Paying attention to nonverbal language is the real life application of reading the fine print. We can avoid signing for a package of trouble if we don't discount the nonverbal, nonlinear, sometimes nonlogical messages that ask for our attention.

Otherwise, prepare for a lot of "experience."

TODAY'S LESSON:

I am aware.

SILENCE

The fruits of silence are self-control, courage, endurance, patience and dignity.

—OHIYESA

Silent things are mighty things. A bud opening into a blossom. The full moon appearing at twilight. The birth of a good idea. A broken bone knitting itself back together. The start of spring. A wave of tenderness. A vivid dream.

These silent and powerful things serve as examples for me. Paying attention to things that don't clamor for my ear or use words to be understood helps me to become less distracted and confused. When I am conscious and silent, I am renewed.

TODAY'S LESSON:
Silence plus awareness gives me strength.

RESPECT

You must not hurt anybody or do harm to anyone. You must not fight.
Do right always. It will give you satisfaction in life.

—WOVOKA

"Hey—don't *dis* me," young people say, meaning don't disrespect me. To disrespect means I *dis*dain you, show *dis*taste for your ways and *dis*gust for your lifestyle. When I *dis*respect, I *dis*criminate against you and keep my *dis*tance from you and wish that you would *dis*appear. What a *dis*grace.

But can we take "dis" to a new level? One where I would *dis*cover your good attributes and try to change my *dis*position in order to *dis*play sympathy and brotherhood. Can we have a *dis*cussion that's open and honest? If so, we could shed our masks and *dis*guises in order to find out what makes each of us *dis*tinctive. We would *dis*allow all negativity. We would become *dis*ciples of love and happiness. A world where everyone behaved that way would be better than living in *Dis*neyland!

TODAY'S LESSON:

I treat students with respect.

LOVE

Why should you take by force from us that which you can obtain by love?

—POWHATAN KING WAHUNSONACOOK

I believe most teachers are motivated by love. Even still, we are authority figures and we sometimes throw our weight around. Inside the classroom, we are rulers of our own private empires. We may come to believe that an iron hand and tight control are the be-all and end-all. Order is necessary, but it should be tempered with the rule of love. Love ultimately yields better results than coercion. Our students—just like anyone else—want to be attended to, delighted in, challenged, cherished, and esteemed. Just like every other human, more than anything else they may need, they need to be loved.

TODAY'S LESSON:

I balance consideration and control.

RELAXATION

*Certain small things and observances sometimes have connection
with large and more profound ideas.*

—PLENTY COUPS

Take a ten-minute vacation. Meditate instead of turning on the TV, play a record and sing along rather than grabbing some junk food to give yourself a boost. Walk to the store instead of driving. Stand up and do some stretches. Write down what's on your mind in a journal. Gaze out the window.

TODAY'S LESSON:
I seek serenity.

JOY

*It is a paradox of creative recovery that we must get
serious about taking ourselves lightly.*

—JULIA CAMERON

The junk food jingle is right. Yes, you do deserve a break today. Sometimes we relax and indulge ourselves and that's a healthy thing. But too often we take the break in an unhealthy way. We're not giving ourselves much of a gift by eating empty calories, watching TV, or reading escapist fiction.

There are other more refreshing ways to have a private recess, to unwind, unknot, and to re-create ourselves. A walk, a phone call to a friend we haven't contacted in a while, a bubble bath. Or what about writing a poem, playing the piano, or doing a quick sketch?

Don't let recess be an outlet that only kids get to enjoy. We may not want to jump double Dutch on the playground or play with an electronic gadget, a ball, or a musical instrument.

Then again, why not?

TODAY'S LESSON:

I can find something fun to do and do it.

GRATITUDE

That's the point. It goes like this. Teaching is touching life.

—JAIME ESCALANTE

What are the beautiful things about teaching? Teaching a lesson that you know really works. Seeing the proverbial lightbulb spark when a child "gets it." Hearing a student's heartfelt thanks. Meeting up with a former student who tells you how you impacted his life. Being a part of the solution and not the pollution or the dissolution of society. Knowing that you are contributing to the uplift of humankind.

TODAY'S LESSON:

I am grateful to be in the midst of such beauty.

DIVERSITY

Not everything that's mainstream is universal.

—JOEL DIAS-PORTER

William Shakespeare—he was the famous army general during World War I, right? Of course not. We know that Shakespeare was the English poet and playwright of Elizabethan England. Everyone knows Shakespeare and he had some good stories to tell, but he's not the only one. There are poets, playwrights, philosophers, and thinkers from peoples in other parts of the world that have important things to share. Right in your very own school there is a teacher from another country, a child who speaks a language other than English at home, a colleague who has a distinctly unique worldview that would enrich you to experience it.

You yourself may be outside the mainstream because of your accent, your appearance, or your outlook. Each of these differences is valuable and beautiful and needs to be known by as many of us as possible. Don't limit yourself—please go and encounter the riches right within reach.

TODAY'S LESSON:

I value diversity.

FEAR

Fear is that little darkroom where negatives are developed.

—MICHAEL PRITCHARD

Swimming was something Tracy couldn't do. Or wouldn't do was more accurate, because Tracy was afraid of the water. Eventually, though, she got tired of sitting on the sidelines at the beach. "Half the kids I teach in class can swim and they think it's fun. If they can do it, so can I," she told herself. "It's time I got over my fear,"

Tracy enrolled in a class for people who were scared of the water. She learned how to splash around just for fun, stick her face in the water, submerge her head in the pool, float face down and on her back. Eventually, she began to take strokes.

The amazing thing is that as she overcame her fear of the water, other situations in her life got clearer. She saw that it was time to change schools. She realized she had a fear of prosperity that made her too grasping about money. She loosened the iron grip she had on her money only to find that income began to flow from unexpected sources. Her annual attack of the flu didn't show up that year, either. Facing just one fear opened the floodgates that washed away other fears.

What are you afraid of? What could you do to conquer a fear that would enlarge your life?

TODAY'S LESSON:

Face everything and recover.

LISTENING

We show respect by simply listening with complete attention.

—EKNATH EASWARAN

The training for the crisis hot line telephone counselors included reflective listening. That is mirroring a client's feelings in a calm and thoughtful tone. Even if a caller is in a rage, the counselor merely tries to identify the feeling and gently reflect the essence of the emotion being expressed back to the caller. For example, a caller may say, "I can't believe he had an affair with another woman!" The listener might reply by saying, "It sounds like you're very angry with your husband," or "I can see you are upset."

During the training sessions, we practiced responding to one another using reflective listening techniques. One person in a pair would role-play an agitated, depressed, or emotionally out-of-control client; the other person would make the listener's response. To do the response, one had to be very focused and work to be completely attentive to the one speaking.

"You know," said my partner, "even though I know we're only play-acting, speaking in this calm, controlled way really is making me feel soothed."

TODAY'S LESSON:

Peace is contagious.

RESPECT

*People will forget what you said, people will forget what you did,
but people will not forget how you made them feel.*

—UNKNOWN

Who was your favorite teacher? What do you remember about that teacher? When asked that question most people talk about how in Mrs. Carmody's class she made learning fun, or they remember how Mr. Jackson's corny jokes made everyone laugh and feel comfortable, or how Miss Sanchez made each person in the room feel special, not just the A students. Seldom do people say "I loved my tenth-grade teacher because she could really work math problems" or "She gained my respect because she had perfect attendance."

What were the qualities of that favorite teacher? The good thing about having a role model is that you can still model the good role that she set even when she is no longer an active part of your life. Pick one of the qualities you admired about your favorite teacher to cultivate in yourself.

TODAY'S LESSON:

I imitate the best of the best and make it my own.

THOUGHTFULNESS

My religion is very simple. My religion is kindness.

—THE DALAI LAMA

It is surprisingly refreshing to do someone a special favor in secret, to be an anonymous angel. If you know a coworker is broke, slip a $10 bill in her purse. Should you overhear a child say he left his lunch at home, go to the cafeteria and pay for his meal in advance. If you notice the parking meter has expired, deposit a few coins to keep the driver from getting a ticket.

The enjoyment of giving is one of the most marvelous features of humankind. Today is a good day to show what kind of human you are.

TODAY'S LESSON:

I will do something good for someone else without anyone knowing it.

ORGANIZATION

To survive, we must begin to know sacredness. The pace which most of us live prevents this.

—CHRYSTOS

With the long list of items on our To-Do List, many of us consider that we live a full and busy life. However, there is a difference between leading a full life and one that is merely busy.

> Full means you're on the right road.
> Busy mean you're on the fast track.
>
> Full means your mind is occupied.
> Busy means your mind is preoccupied.
>
> Full means your life is balanced.
> Busy means your life is a balancing act.
>
> Full means serenity.
> Busy means insanity.

TODAY'S LESSON:

I will eliminate some things from my busy schedule
so my life can be full.

TRUTH

It is important that students bring a certain ragamuffin barefoot irreverence
to their studies; they are not here to worship what is known, but to question it.

—JACOB BRONOWSKI

You think you know a lot of things, and you probably do. The tricky part is that some of what you know to be true is false. At one time medical science "knew" that using leeches for bloodletting was a good cure. At one time, teachers "knew" that rote memorization was the best technique for learning. At one time, everybody "knew" that the world was flat.

At some level, your students know that some of what you are teaching them is not true. And much of what may be truth now won't remain true tomorrow.

TODAY'S LESSON:

The truth is born in inquiring minds.

SERVICE

It is better to give and *receive.*

—BERNARD GUNTHER

Helping can feel like a dangerous act. Not everyone who needs help wants it. Not everyone who wants help gets it. Helping can make both parties to the helping transaction feel uncomfortable. Some of us feel more comfortable with only one side. Our pride makes us reluctant to receive help. We are natural givers and often don't want to receive help—our overdeveloped independence prevents us from allowing others to show concern and to demonstrate care. Or our self-absorption blocks us from seeing the need around us. We like to get help but seldom think of extending ourselves for the other guy.

Working only one side of the exchange makes our personalities lopsided. The beauty about helping is its two-sided nature. The helper can't help without being enhanced, too. And the helped one gets what is needed plus he or she gets to experience fellowship. Genuine giving enlarges the soul and narrows the ego of both parties.

TODAY'S LESSON:

I am willing to give and receive help.

FLEXIBILITY

Men must be born and reborn to belong.

—CHIEF LUTHER STANDING BEAR

Life is like trying to catch a river between your fingers; it gushes and rushes beyond the fixed point where you try to grasp it. The stream of life is a swift current that brings change and even when the change is anticipated, it brings the unexpected into the mix.

There is a limit to how much you can prepare for tomorrow and there are some challenges for which there is no practical way to be ready when they hit. The best we can do is observe the river and take a lesson from it. Go with the flow.

TODAY'S LESSON:

I do the best I can regardless of the circumstances.

REST

He who finds no way to rest cannot long survive the battle.

—JAMES BALDWIN

Mr. Kramer was on every school committee, had a full teaching load, and led the drama club after school. He was a jazz aficionado who played with a band on the side. He had a wife, a son, a daughter, and a dog. "When do you find time to sleep?" friends asked him.

"I sleep fast," he'd quip and then was off to the next activity. During the summer, he never took a vacation. He always had a summer job lined up. Occasionally he would take a weekend trip but always combined it with business. "When do you find time to relax?" folks would ask him.

"Can't make money relaxing," he quipped.

One day he didn't show up for work. He ended up being off for six weeks—sick in the bed, unable to move. All that extra money went for medicine and medical treatments. All those projects on which he felt he was indispensable were done by other people. It's admirable to be active and involved in the world, but if you don't learn to take a chill pill, you'll end up with a doctor's bill.

TODAY'S LESSON:

My schedule is not complete if I don't make time to rest.

HUMILITY

Life is a long lesson in humility.

—JAMES BARRIE

I was at the bank handling a routine transaction when I noticed a good-looking twenty-something looking at me. He wasn't merely looking, he was staring, eying me up and down with great interest.

"Yeah, I still got it," I thought to myself smugly. "I still turn heads."

When I walked out the door, I felt a hand on my shoulder. "Don't I know you?" the young man asked me. It was an old line, but as cute as he was, I was willing to let it work on me.

"Well, you do look familiar," I responded, truthfully. Was he one of my neighbors?

"Didn't you teach at Brookland School?" he asked. I had worked there nearly fifteen years ago. When I confirmed that I had, he spoke in that tone of voice reserved only for elders, "Don't you remember me? You taught me in the fifth grade."

Oh.

TODAY'S LESSON:

I keep my ego in check.

INSIGHT

If you hate a person you hate something in him that is a part of yourself.
What isn't part of ourselves doesn't disturb us.

—HERMANN HESSE

The people you dislike have faces like mirrors. That is to say, when you look at them you see an aspect of yourself reflected. The reason the class clown grates on your nerves is that you see the insecurity that he covers with loud jokes and foolish behavior is the same anxiety you work hard to hide. In your opinion, the vice principal has more vices than principles because you two share some of the same character flaws.

The next time you find yourself around someone who rubs you the wrong way, it may be your cue to scratch below the surface and see what that reveals about you.

TODAY'S LESSON:

I am willing to recognize my shortcomings.

INTEGRITY

Only our concept of time makes it possible for us to speak of the Day of Judgment by that name; in reality it is a summary court in perpetual session.

—FRANZ KAFKA

Many students dread report card day, thinking of it as a stressful day when teachers hand out criticism and parents mete out punishment. They are unable to see that the grade on the paper is the result of weeks and months of poor behavior and unfinished assignments. Students take a test and feel that they're lucky if they get an A and unfairly penalized by a teacher who dislikes them if the grade is low. How well or how much they studied doesn't figure that highly into their equation.

It's the same with us. We "can't understand" why awful things keep happening to us—"Why is God making me His favorite victim—I haven't done anything!" It's true—life does present unexpected quirks and quandaries and no one can guarantee the future. Bad things do happen to good people and sometimes the wicked prosper while decent folks suffer. But this is also true—there are an abundance of situations wherein the good things we do result in good outcomes and the bad things we do have adverse effects.

We don't live our lives in a vacuum. Our thoughts and actions touch others and reverberate to ourselves. We may not see all the associations clearly, or decode every cause and effect, but those connections are there.

TODAY'S LESSON:

Everything is connected to everything else.

COMMUNICATION

Life is a foreign language. All men mispronounce it.

—CHRISTOPHER MORLEY

A native English-speaking fifth grader was teasing a Hispanic girl. He ran to his teacher and said that Maria had called him a bad word. Maria denied it and insisted that Mark had been teasing her even though she had tried to make him leave her alone. But Mark was insistent that Maria had insulted him by calling him a bastard.

About a month later, this teacher enrolled in a Spanish class because an increasing number of her students were children from Central America. One day during the class, the Spanish instructor asked the group to settle down. *"¡Basta! ¡Basta! No habla, por favor.* Stop, stop talking, please."

"Basta!" The lightbulb came on. *Basta* is what the little girl had said to the boy. Stop. *Basta*—not bastard. They had had a miscommunication.

TODAY'S LESSON:

I make an extra effort to understand the other person.

INTUITION

The only tyrant I accept in this world is the still, small voice within me.

—MAHATMA GANDHI

There is a guide on the inside that will tell us what to do in a given situation if we are able to hear it. Being able to hear it usually requires three things: that we still our souls, have an attitude of receptivity, and have a willingness to entertain something new and different.

These three things are not small things to accomplish. A still soul is continually tempted to be a busybody by attention to attractive distractions—work to do, children to attend to, friends in need, fatigue, fun. Then when we have cleared our calendars and quieted our minds, we must be open, expectant, patient for the message to arrive in its own time and way. Too often waiting turns to worry or restless boredom and we bail out before the message manifests.

Finally, once the message has come, it may prove so different from what we expected, we reject it out of hand. And it's true—what that still, small whisper is urging us to do will probably be an unusual idea, a new truth, a pointer toward a path we've never thought about taking.

It may scare us to obey that voice. It may be a challenge to follow it. It may prove hard to follow through. But in nearly every case and circumstance, not to honor it means disaster.

TODAY'S LESSON:
I thoughtfully obey inner guidance.

ACTION

Children have more need of models than of critics.

—JOSEPH JOUBERT

What grown-up did you admire when you were young? Chances are you were drawn by how the individual carried himself or herself, an encouraging word offered, a courageous act you saw done. It's extremely doubtful that the person you looked up to was someone who constantly criticized you.

Even as adults, we prefer to be around people who have more "do-so" than "say-so." Nags are a drag on the spirit. People who are walking the walk are too busy living life to spend much time finding fault.

What do students see when they observe you? Someone who tells them to "do as I say, not as I do"? Or someone worthy of respect and emulation?

TODAY'S LESSON:

My actions speak louder than my words.

PERSPECTIVE

Remember friends as you go by,
As you are now, so once was I,
As I am now, so you must be.
Prepare yourself to follow me.

—COMMON EIGHTEENTH-CENTURY EPITAPH

One day it will all be over: the comments and complaints we have about the school and the students, the business of correcting papers and misbehaving children, the hustle and bustle, the happiness and headache. Ten years from now it will be remembered as the good old days. Fifty years from now it won't be remembered at all. One hundred years from now, we will all be dead.

Is it worth the energy we're wasting on it? Decide what's important and devote your energy to that. Evaluate it by these things: Does it increase the peace? Does it foster understanding? Does it promote learning? Does it support healthy relationships? Will it bring about healthy change? Is it life or death?

TODAY'S LESSON:

I put my problems in perspective.

SILENCE

If you are a beginning teacher, listen, listen, listen.
If you are an experienced teacher, listen, listen, listen.

—HARRY K. WONG AND ROSEMARY WONG

My colleagues and I were leading a large teacher training institute. The topic was how to best teach immigrant children, and the discussion was lively. I was enjoying hearing the opinions and comments of some of the more forceful and articulate participants but my cofacilitator noted something wrong.

"Please," she said, "for the next twenty minutes could we allow someone else to speak?"

As I looked out on the faces, I could see the "leaders" in the group bursting with the desire to speak, but they refrained. There was a long stretch of time when nothing was said. But eventually, in that silent void emerged the voice of a Central American woman, an educational aide who would normally be shy about speaking because of her accent. But her perception was totally different from the ones held by the American workers and it was a view that needed to be heard. Without the encouragement by the facilitator, and the space she created for this new voice to be heard, that valuable insight might have been lost.

There's a student in your class who needs you to provide that same space.

TODAY'S LESSON:

I honor the power of silence.

DECISION MAKING

Indecision is like the stepchild: if he doesn't wash his hands, he is called "dirty,"
if he does, he is wasting the water.

—MADAGASCAN PROVERB

There is never a time when all the facts are in, when every alternative can be tried and every expert consulted before you decide. Most times, if you do the wrong thing, you can correct the mistake. But languishing in the in-between creates distress.

Take all the appropriate preliminary steps: list the pros and cons of both sides of the argument, discuss the issue with a colleague, sit quietly and reflect on the matter. But then comes the time when you must choose.

TODAY'S LESSON:

I think before I act, then I act.

MONEY

From birth to 18 a girl needs good parents. From age 18 to 35 she needs good looks.
From age 35 to 55 she needs a good personality and from 55 on she needs cash.

—SOPHIE TUCKER

"The school system doesn't pay teachers any money," said one teacher to his colleague. "I never have enough. I wish I could meet someone who's doing more than just scraping by."

"I've managed to save a year's income," said the other teacher.

The first teacher was stunned. How could anyone exist on a teacher's salary, much less accumulate any significant sum?

But it can be done. It behooves you to do it. How well we manage our money is not so much a matter of amount but of attitude. No, you probably won't get rich teaching. But you can save a portion of what you do earn.

If it's nothing more than salvaging the change in the bottom of your purse each day and putting it in a jar, you can start handling money in less wasteful ways. There are books and other resources you can consult to learn how to do so.

TODAY'S LESSON:

Managing money prudently is my responsibility.

KNOWLEDGE

The beautiful thing about learning is nobody can take it away from you.

—B. B. KING

If your home and possessions went up in flames, what would be left? The piece of paper that was your high school diploma would be nothing but ashes, but the things you learned in school would help you to reconstruct your life. The shop class where you learned how to wield a hammer and nails would help you build a new house. The English class where you learned to read and comprehend would help you to interpret your homeowner's insurance policy.

As teachers, we are giving students the building blocks for the foundations of their future lives. What you present in class may be the bit of information that allows escape from danger, prevents someone from being cheated in a business deal, or helps somebody land or keep a job.

We have an obligation to give our students building blocks made of solid substance that will be the infrastructure of a good life. We are giving them the foundation that will stand when everything else is gone.

TODAY'S LESSON:

I recognize the importance of my work.

CREATIVITY

You are made in the image of your Creator so you have no choice but to be creative.
Anything less is a sin.

—JOY JONES

Being creative is not just a luxury. It's a spiritual mandate. A woman discovered she had a tumor growing on her ovary. One morning while meditating about the matter, she sensed a message from within. *The reason you have this tumor is that you've blocked your creativity.*

Being creative doesn't necessarily mean you have to draw pictures or sing an operatic aria. It may mean bringing more verve and enthusiasm to the task at hand. It could mean following an offbeat thought wherever it leads. It might mean asking one's students how they'd like to proceed and changing the lesson accordingly. Don't think of it as extra work but as an extra opportunity to bring healing or to become healed.

TODAY'S LESSON:

I am a channel of creative energy.

COURAGE

Life shrinks or expands in proportion to one's courage.

—ANAÏS NIN

"I became an editor," a woman told me, "because I really wanted to be a writer, but I was scared to admit that I really wanted to write." By working around words and around writers, this woman tried to pacify the urge to do what she truly longed to do by way of a vicarious path. You can be lost although you're in the right neighborhood. But being in the right neighborhood is not the same as being on the right road.

Perhaps you are a teacher because it puts you in the company of youth—people who are alive, questioning, unbound by convention—is there a part of your soul that wishes it was more alive, yearns to take up a quest, and wants to be unconventional? Do you work around children because there is a part of you that wants a safe space to play? Or is it time to stop playing it safe? Is there a part of you that hasn't grown up? Or that wants to grow out in a different direction?

You don't necessarily have to quit teaching, but you may need to quit pretending that there isn't a part of your soul that needs to dance.

TODAY'S LESSON:

Take a creative risk.

JOY

Be happy while you're living, for you're a long time dead.

—SCOTTISH PROVERB

Do you need permission to do what you've always wanted to do? Well, today you've got it. Fill in the following permission slip.

I, _____, grant myself permission to try
        (your name)

something new and wonderful. This wonderful activity will

take place on _____. The thing I
                    (date)

want to do is: _____.

TODAY'S LESSON:

I commit to doing one wonderful thing.

DESIRE

A man ought to desire that which is genuine instead of that which is artificial.

—OKUTE

The word "desire," broken down into its parts "de" and "sire," means "of" the "Father," suggesting that our deep wants have a divine origin. With this supreme and compelling source animating the things we want passionately, we are assured of achieving them.

So what is it that we desire? If our focus is on cars, clothes, and cuties, we may attain them but still feel unfulfilled and unsatisfied.

What would happen if you desired to be an inspiring teacher, an effective parent, a compassionate human? Take your desire to a deeper level.

TODAY'S LESSON:

I harness my desires for good.

GOAL SETTING

*I find television very educating. Every time somebody turns on the set,
I go into the other room and read a book.*

—GROUCHO MARX

Overheard in the teachers' lounge:

"You don't have cable? Well, I can get you connected at a very reasonable rate."

"No thanks, I'm not interested."

"What—you don't *want* cable? Why not?"

"Spending more time watching television is not one of my goals in life. If I watch a lot of TV, I won't have time to do some of the things I really want to do."

What are your real goals? Would turning off the television be helpful in reaching them?

TODAY'S LESSON:

I limit the time I spend watching television.

INTUITION

A hunch is creativity trying to tell you something.

—FRANK CAPRA

There's a nagging thought that haunts you. It keeps coming back like a recurring dream. It whispers, "Don't do that" or "Take the other road." It may tell you to "Call Mr. Romero," or "Drive home the long way," or "Although it didn't work the last time, try it once more."

Don't ignore that sensation because it means you're about to hurtle ahead, surmount an obstacle, create something splendid, escape a close call, achieve a breakthrough, take a leap of faith.

TODAY'S LESSON:

I pay attention to my intuition.

FOCUS

Misplaced emphasis occurs . . . when you think that everything is going well because your car drives so smoothly and your new suit fits you so well, and those high-priced shoes you bought make your feet feel so good; and you begin to believe that these things, these many luxuries all around, are the really important matters of your life.

—MARTIN LUTHER KING SR.

So you want to be a millionaire? Just what would you do with a million dollars? Many people would use the money to start over. All the things they've been waiting to do until . . . they'd start today. They would use the money to help them meet influential people. They would find ways to follow their dreams and set new goals.

I hate to be the one to tell you, but you probably won't win a million dollars. But that doesn't mean you can't start over. It doesn't mean you can't follow your dreams or set new goals. You can always change your attitude. That one change alone is guaranteed to set new and wonderful things in motion.

To be sure, it is good to have cash in the bank. But if you have a decent attitude and a willingness to work, life can be good and can continue to get better even if you aren't a millionaire.

TODAY'S LESSON:

I give my attention to the important matters in my life.

PEACE

Learn to be quiet enough to hear the sound of the genuine within yourself so that you can hear it in other people.

—MARIAN WRIGHT EDELMAN

Parents can be extremely rude and irate. They call the school upset about an "unreasonable" school policy, an "incompetent" schoolteacher, or the "totally corrupt" school system. Whether or not their concerns are well founded, not matching the vexed parent's decibel level goes a long way to keep the tension from escalating.

Many times the upset other person wants to know—wants to *feel*—that his or her side of the argument is truly heard. Your calm tone helps the parent to realize that agitation is not synonymous with action and that expressing anger is not the same as demanding respect.

TODAY'S LESSON:

I model serenity.

THOUGHTFULNESS

Happiness is the natural by-product of favoring another with loving attention.

—KAREN CASEY

Beverly and I always exchanged birthday and Christmas presents. Then she moved about fifty miles away. When gift-giving time rolled around, I'd still buy her a present, but by the time we could synchronize our schedules and I could pay her a visit, Christmas was a season or two in the past or the birthday was months gone by. That meant I might receive a package decorated with snowflakes during spring break. Or my birthday card would arrive three months before the next birthday.

The result of this eccentric timing is that on an otherwise blah and ordinary day, I'd get an unexpected surprise. Or sometimes on an absolutely miserable day, a cheery gift would show up and totally rescue my mood from the garbage pail.

There is someone in your life who would benefit from a "no special occasion" greeting card, gift, phone call, or personal letter.

TODAY'S LESSON:

Today is the day to do something kind and unexpected.

GRATITUDE

Not what we have, but what we enjoy constitutes our abundance.

—LINDA COONS

My baby nephew loves dirt. Whether it's sand in a sandbox, soil in a garden, or dust on the sidewalk, he revels in the sensation of tiny grains sifting through his fingers and exclaims at the hills, peaks, and swirls he can create with it. A walk around the block takes an hour because he insists on stopping every few steps to play with a pile of dirt. Something as commonplace as dirt is an occasion for joy for Robert. Because there is so much dirt around (both outdoors and inside the house) he's always happy.

Would that we would take joy in the extremely ordinary things around us. We may never own a luxury plane—or even a luxury car. We can't count on being chosen Teacher of the Year or writing a Pulitzer Prize winner. Teachers can't necessarily count on getting a cost-of-living raise next year.

But we can take pleasure in a good night's sleep, a congenial conversation among friends, a parking space near the door, a short line at the store, a cold drink on a hot day, the smell of a fresh box of crayons, the feel of rain falling on the face—even in dirt.

TODAY'S LESSON:
The plain and ordinary are delightful.

MONEY

I had plastic surgery last week. I cut up my credit cards.

—HENNY YOUNGMAN

It was on sale, so I had to buy
Couldn't let that bargain pass me by
All it takes to have the style deluxe
Is to part with a few extra bucks
At every store in the local mall
I came, I charged, I bought it all
At home, on-line, I shop and click
Choose it now, ship it quick
Because of all these consumer cravings
I have absolutely zilch in my savings.

TODAY'S LESSON:

Even if it's only $10, I will set aside a portion of my pay for savings.

GRATITUDE

You never miss the water till the well goes dry.
You'll never miss your baby till she says good-bye.

—BLUES LYRIC

There's plenty to complain about if you're a teacher. Overcrowded classes, a shortage of supplies, nonsupportive administrators, apathetic parents, leaky roofs, a temperamental photocopier . . . and the list goes on.

We may complain and whine when our classes are overcrowded, but worry and wail if enrollment drops and the board of education threatens to close the school down. Suddenly, a room full of students seems like a grand idea.

Why wait till the tables turn before we appreciate the things in our lives? There are things about teaching that are absolutely wonderful, making it more gratifying than most jobs. At the very least, it is an honorable way to make a living.

TODAY'S LESSON:

I appreciate what I have.

ACTION

Take time to deliberate, but when the time for action arrives, stop thinking and go in.

—ANDREW JACKSON

Suppose you were in New York and you had to get to Florida but didn't know how to get there. If you just started driving with no directions, you would probably get lost. You would have to ask for directions, and it would take you some time to make the trek, but you would get there. On the other hand, you could start the trip by making elaborate preparations. You could write to the Miami Chamber of Commerce for brochures, interview people who had been to Florida before, consult a map, and study it carefully. Why not even study cartography and draw a map of your own? You could make so many preparations that you would never leave home. To be sure, traveling without a clue is not the most efficient way to go, but at least you will reach your destination.

Be a trail maker, not a mapmaker. Bon voyage!

TODAY'S LESSON:

It's time to to do something.

CHANGE

*If you do not re-verse your ways of thinking, speaking and doing,
you will remain on the wheel of no motion.*

—RALPHA

If you aren't careful, you may turn into a tent caterpillar. Tent caterpillars travel by following the silken thread left by the caterpillar ahead of them. If the lead caterpillar inadvertently catches sight of the thread left by the last caterpillar, the caterpillars will march in an unending circle. One procession of caterpillars was observed marching in a circle for over a week.

How long have you been walking in circles?

TODAY'S LESSON:

It is time to break the cycle.

INSTRUCTION

Our goal is not so much the imparting of knowledge as the unveiling and developing of spiritual energy.

—MARIA MONTESSORI

A boy was asked by the principal about his academic progress—or rather, the lack thereof. "Son, are you the laziest person in the class?" asked the educator.

"What do you mean by 'lazy'?" asked the boy.

"You know what lazy is," the principal said, irritated. "Think about what goes on in your class. When everyone else is busy studying the book or writing papers, who is it that sits back watching everybody else work hard?"

"The teacher."

TODAY'S LESSON:

I am an involved teacher.

SUCCESS

Success doesn't lead to a positive attitude, a positive attitude leads to success.

—KEITH BOYKIN

Good outcomes result from good work and good luck. Good work comes from good skills and good working relationships; good luck comes from having good timing. Good timing comes from having a good instinct for being in the right place at the right time. Having good instincts is not a conscious process; it comes from having a generally good outlook on life, which proceeds from a good inner life. A good inner life starts with a good attitude. It all starts with attitude.

TODAY'S LESSON:

I have a positive attitude.

TIMING

The world is not happening to us. We are happening to it.

—IYANLA VANZANT

We think of good timing as a lightning strike—it hits once and then it's gone. But sometimes opportunity strikes twice.

We know the name Spalding as the athletic supply company. The founder, Albert Goodwill Spalding, as may be expected, loved sports. As a young man, he knew he could pitch. The baseball scouts knew it, too, and offered the high schooler a $2,500 contract to sign with one of the baseball teams in New York, Cleveland, or Washington, D.C. This was in the 1860s and Spalding was a seventeen-year-old earning $5 a week as a grocery store clerk. The offers were a terrific opportunity but Spalding's mother had reservations, so he turned them down.

Instead, Spalding took work as a bookkeeper. Over the next five years he worked at seven different businesses—and each one went bankrupt. This caused Spalding to wonder . . .

Finally, in 1871, he decided to pursue his original dream. He became a pitcher for the Boston Red Stockings. He maintained the high batting average of .320 and was key in leading the Boston Red Stockings to win four pennants between 1872 and 1875.

Sometimes you misinterpret the sign the first time, but when life sends the signal again will you seize it?

TODAY'S LESSON:

I reexamine my options.

COURAGE

Sometimes courage has to take the place of faith.

—SUSAN SHAUGHNESSY

I've read that it is more exhausting to stand for an hour than to walk for an hour. Inaction may seem like a less hazardous path, but moving forward is less dangerous than being a sitting duck.

Faith is trusting that things will ultimately turn out well, even when present circumstances look pretty bleak. Courage is recognizing that yes, things are pretty perilous yet mustering up the nerve to go forward anyway—without any guarantees of a happy ending. Courage isn't going forward without fear. It means going forward fear and all.

TODAY'S LESSON:
I step forward in spite of my fears.

FAILURE

A setback is a set up for a comeback.

—WILLIE JOLLEY

"We don't think they will do anything in their market. Guitar groups are on their way out," wrote someone at a recording company that took a pass on the Beatles in 1962.

He went bankrupt twice, had a nervous breakdown, and lost seven political campaigns before Abraham Lincoln became president of the United States.

The best-sellers *Member of the Wedding, The Ballad of the Sad Café,* and *The Heart Is a Lonely Hunter* plus more were written by Carson McCullers, who suffered two strokes before she turned thirty, the suicide of her husband, partial paralysis, and chronic pain. Nonetheless, she committed to writing at least one page daily, no matter what.

TODAY'S LESSON:
I hurdle my problems and keep going.

DRESS

Beauty is only skin-deep, but it's only the skin you see.

—A. PRICE

A lot of schools have instituted dress codes. The student body may have to adhere to strict guidelines for proper school attire. Other schools require uniforms. The philosophy behind both approaches is that appearance influences attitude.

Your appearance also influences your students' attitudes. A professional appearance makes more than just a "fashion statement." It tells your class and your coworkers that you come to school ready to work and that you think enough of yourself—and them—to put in the extra time to be presentable.

I have noticed that when I'm dressed neatly, there seem to be fewer behavior problems. It's almost as if students adjust their behavior to fit in with the message my clothing projects. How we dress is part of the classroom climate.

TODAY'S LESSON:
I am a competent, caring teacher and I look the part.

HEALTH

The most sacred place isn't the Church, the Mosque or the temple,
it's the temple of the body. That's where the spirit lives.

—SUSAN TAYLOR

How should you treat your best friend? How do you care for the one who will be with you no matter what? How well do you love that intimate one who reads your mind and responds to your innermost thoughts, who hurts when you hurt and bears all your pains? That unique and wonderful one is your body and should be cherished and appreciated as the special love of your life. Do you refresh your body with lots of water and nourish it with healthy food? Do you give it ample opportunity to stretch, run, play, and move? Does it receive its proper rest? Get to know your body and its needs. Treat it as if it were the nearest and dearest friend you could ever know. Act as if you would just die if it ever left you. Unlike some of the lovers you have known, if you love your body, it will love you back.

TODAY'S LESSON:

I will eat a healthy meal, drink water, and exercise today.

DIVERSITY

My upbringing taught us that cultures are not related, and perish when deprived of contact with what is different and challenging.

—CARLOS FUENTES

Today's classrooms don't merely reflect the community, they reflect the world. Some big-city school systems have over one hundred languages represented in the student population. With the mix of cultures coming together—or sometimes colliding—everyone is forced to stretch in order to accommodate the unfamiliar. Signs appear in both English and Spanish. Debates rage about how best to welcome and instruct immigrant students. Cherished school traditions are questioned or even discarded.

We sometimes resent these changes, feeling that the cross-cultural exchange cultivates more struggle than sympathy and more friction than fellowship. We need to remember what we learned in biology—that cross-fertilization enhances the growth and development of plants. It enhances the growth and development of other living things, too. Like humans.

TODAY'S LESSON:
I embrace diversity.

LOVE

Remember, to hate, to be violent, is demeaning. It means you're afraid of the other side of the coin, to love and be loved.

—JAMES BALDWIN

The fearful part of loving is that it comes with complications. It urges us to give more than seems safe, to care in a way that seems foolish, to be true to our calling, to exert power in a way that is so mighty, we fear we may abuse it. Safer to be a victim or a victimizer than to be vulnerable, or so we rationalize.

It is possible to be vulnerable without either getting too damaged or doing too much damage, but most of us are too frightened to take that chance. We choose fright over insight and being cool over being real. But to be both godlike and childlike all at once is to be so very gloriously human.

TODAY'S LESSON:

I choose love over fear.

CHANGE

The best thing for a sluggish mind is to disturb the routine.

—WILLIAM DANFORTH

Perhaps your brain needs a change of scenery. You don't have to travel to a foreign country or get an additional degree to get a fresh perspective. The only passport needed is to shift the routine a little in order to reroute the traffic patterns of your typical thinking. If you normally drive, take public transportation to work. If you usually ride the bus, get off a stop earlier and walk. Read a magazine you wouldn't normally read. (Just to get started, pick up a copy of *Opera News, Gramophone, Arthritis Today,* or *Arabian Horse World.*) Invite someone you don't know well to join you for lunch. Ask someone with an unusual job to speak to the class.

Taking an imaginative mental detour may unjam a psychic gridlock you didn't even realize was blocking traffic. When we free our minds to experiment with new arrangements and departures from the norm, the results can be provocative combinations that will invigorate our lessons, maybe even transform our lives.

TODAY'S LESSON:

I try something new.

ACCEPTANCE

Rap's the voice and expression of the street. There's got to be negative; there's got to be positive. Gotta be up, down, yin and yang. Day and night. It all fits together.

—KID FROST

Young people are so engaging, so rewarding to be with when they are learning and responding. But when that positive energy swings to its opposite pole and we have to confront a sullen teen or separate students in a fight, we wish we could do something to contain them.

However, you can't separate the mischief from the marvelous, the mirth from the hurt. And we don't really want a room full of "Stepford students" who do everything we ask them to do, do we? Even if we do want it, it's impossible to separate and keep only the "good" parts. We have to subscribe to it all. You can't have birdsong without bird droppings or sweet-smelling flowers without sunshine . . . and rain.

TODAY'S LESSON:

I accept the whole of life.

LOVE

However broken down the spirit's shrine, the spirit is there all the same.

—NIGERIAN PROVERB

There are some people I just don't like. No matter how tolerant I try to be, they still rub me the wrong way. There are some students who just refuse to do right. It doesn't matter whether I ask them nicely or use my mean teacher voice, they are perverse in their desire to be contrary.

But—no matter how ugly the attitude a person may display—he or she is still a beautiful creation of God. Though hard to tell from the outside, somewhere inside there is a precious human spirit. No matter how impossible and incredible it seems, no one is totally unlovable. No matter what, my mission is always to try and show love just the same.

TODAY'S LESSON:

I honor the beautiful spirit inside each person.

HUMILITY

Few [are] too young, and none too old, to make the attempt to learn.

—BOOKER T. WASHINGTON

Freddy was quite a guy. The first day of class this twelve-year-old asked me what my credentials were for teaching creative writing. I told him I had written a book. He told me he was an author, too, and pulled out the four-page crayon-illustrated story he had written. "I'll sell it to you for a dollar," he told me and I bought it.

The second week of class, Freddy asked me what had I written. I reminded him that I had authored a book. "Haven't you written anything else since?" he asked. A few weeks later, he asked me the same thing again. Although I didn't say anything to him, I was offended. Who was this little boy to be questioning me about my work as if he were some authority figure? But the more I thought about it, I realized that Freddy was doing me a service. How many classes had I taken for that very purpose—to have an authority figure prod me into continuing to write? How many times had I paid for someone to coach or counsel me regarding my career? Here was Freddy doing it for me for free. I adjusted my attitude and got to work on my next project.

TODAY'S LESSON:

My students have lessons to teach me.

ENTHUSIASM

Exuberance is beauty.

—WILLIAM BLAKE

Almost nothing is more delightful and inspiring than being around someone who genuinely enjoys his or her work. Whether it's a child who is excited about learning or a teacher who loves teaching, just being in the presence of someone like that converts the more jaded among us by their joy.

The word "enthusiasm" derives from the terms "en" and "theos," meaning "in God." When we are enthusiastic about a task, we are captivated by a beautiful spirit. Become a disciple of zest and a believer in zeal.

TODAY'S LESSON:

I will find at least one thing about my job to be
happy about and show it.

CREATIVITY

Why should we all use our creative power . . . ? Because there is nothing that makes people so generous, joyful, lively, bold and compassionate, so indifferent to fighting and the accumulation of objects and money.

—BRENDA UELAND

We know how to define the arts—they're painting, dancing, singing. But we also use the term art to describe the practice of other disciplines when we want to acknowledge that there is something more than calculation and technical competency needed in the execution of a job. We speak of the art of playing baseball or the art of carpentry. Or we say there's an art to writing proposals or programming a computer.

151

When we are obedient to the art of teaching, we come to the job charged and energized. We don't merely inform, we are able to inspire. And that kind of inspired communication is communicable—we infect ourselves even as we spread inspiration to others. Wholly engaged in our work, we have less time for criticizing, complaining, or worrying. We work harder but with less fatigue. Bringing all our creativity and talent to bear fills us, frees us, and give us a mystic edge.

TODAY'S LESSON:

I practice the art of teaching.

INGENUITY

At first people refuse to believe that a strange new thing can be done, then they begin to hope it can't be done, then they see it can be done—then it is done and all the world wonders why it was not done centuries before.

—FRANCES HODGSON BURNETT

Karl Benz had developed a three-wheeled motor wagon. But in Germany of 1888, the automobile was still regarded as a silly and dangerous contraption. There was a law that held Herr Benz responsible for any accidents the car caused. As a result, he rarely took his car out of his workshop and when he did, it was only to take it around the block. It was his adventuresome wife, Berta, who decided to take the car on a fifty-nine-mile trip. She took her two sons with her to see their grandmother. In the course of the trip she discovered that the car, with its three-horsepower engine, had only two gears, which wasn't enough to pull itself up a hill. She made a note to add another gear and more horsepower as her boys pushed the car up the slope. As they continued the journey she discovered the car's other shortcomings and improvised spur-of-the-moment remedies to compensate for these problems, which led to ideas that Karl could later refine in his workshop. The novelty of seeing a woman and her two children driving through the countryside headed toward Grandmother's place attracted attention and goodwill to the idea of automotive travel. Berta Benz's risky adventure helped others—including her inventor husband—see this new invention as more than just a "plaything for the rich." Her vision helped make a "silly idea" practical.

TODAY'S LESSON:
Take a chance on a good idea.

ORGANIZATION

Planning is the only way to keep yourself on track. And when you know where you are going, the universe will clear a path for you.

—IYANLA VANZANT

Efficient teachers establish a protocol for helping the class get to work. This may be a written list of guidelines posted on the board, assigned seating so that everyone knows automatically where to sit, or an unspoken expectation about settling down and starting one's seat work that everyone understands.

These procedures help make the class flow smoothly and begin on time. We're able to get students on task, but how about our own lives? Could our personal affairs benefit from a "settle-down" routine? When things start to get a little hectic, frantic, or traumatic, do you have a method for helping yourself to get back on track?

TODAY'S LESSON:

I will develop a personal procedure for putting myself on task.

JOY

The trouble with the rat race is that even if you win, you're still a rat.

—LILY TOMLIN

What was the last time you felt joy?

Perhaps it was the time you played with your toddler; the moment the "Aha!" happened with a student; the day you proposed and the answer was "yes"; getting back into your studio to paint after a long hiatus; singing in the choir, in the shower, in the car.

Make a list of those things that have brought you joy over the last five years. Coming up with a list will tell you something about how to make room for more of these kinds of moments.

If you can't come up with a list, that will tell you something, too.

TODAY'S LESSON:

I do things that bring me joy.

PERSPECTIVE

We don't see things as they are, we see them as we are.

—ANAÏS NIN

A teacher gave permission to two girls to play in the garden adjacent to the school yard. After a few minutes, one girl rushed back indoors crying.

"What is it?" the teacher asked.

"I just saw the rosebush and it's all covered with thorns!" she wailed.

A few minutes later, the other girl raced in. She, too, was excited, but squealing with delight.

"What is it?" asked the teacher.

"I just saw that all the thornbushes come with pretty roses!"

TODAY'S LESSON:

I adopt a positive outlook.

ENCOURAGEMENT

Kind words can be short and easy to speak but their echoes are truly endless.

—MOTHER TERESA

Have you praised a child today? Look through this list and choose a method you haven't tried recently, and give a child the emotional equivalent of free candy. If you really want to be an angel—do the same thing for an adult, too.

- Tell someone "You did a great job!"
- Make a handmade thank-you note
- Post a student's work in a prominent place
- Go to a dollar store and buy a present
- Write a letter to a parent or a boss praising the person
- Slip a $10 or $20 bill in someone's pocket

TODAY'S LESSON:

It gives me joy to spread joy.

ACTION

The ark was built by amateurs and the Titanic *by the experts. Don't wait for the experts.*

—MURRAY COHEN

Okay, so you don't have a degree in that particular specialty. Perhaps your background is in instruction and curriculum but you have a suggestion that pertains to counseling. Or although every year since the school started you've been the sponsor of the drama club, you want to work with the math club this term.

Sometimes we come up with great ideas and other times a great idea will choose us to put it into effect. It may be so offbeat or so grand you think that you can't do it. You *can* do it. As educators, we have a bias for books and degrees but as worthwhile as they are, they don't represent the whole picture. Desire and hard work are just as important as formal education—probably more so. There is a change that needs you to make it happen. Book learning and formal education have their place but nothing surpasses a person with passion and purpose.

TODAY'S LESSON:

I will take a risk on a good idea.

SUCCESS

It's lonely at the top . . . So you'd better know why you're there.

—JOHN MAXWELL

I was surprised to learn that success has its downside. For example, if you have wealth, friends may get upset or jealous if you are not generous in sharing your good fortune with them. And if you *are* generous, some may think you're trying to show off. When you're named Employee of the Month or Teacher of the Year, or the boss simply gives you a pat on the back, your coworkers may become envious of your success.

That's why some of us fear success. We sense some of the negative vibes that often accompany good fortune.

There's nothing inherently wrong with earning money or accolades, although these things are not very satisfying in and of themselves if they are our sole goals. Should we gain them, it helps if the climb to the peak is rooted in relationships and girded by principles that guide our decisions and help us maintain perspective. That way, success will allow us to have self-respect, even if it doesn't bring popularity.

TODAY'S LESSON:

I face success with courage.

TRANQUILITY

Sitting for a set period of time, with no work flowing feels . . . unproductive.
But is it? Your unconscious is paying close attention. It knows that you are honoring it . . .
The payoff will not be withheld forever.

—SUSAN SHAUGHNESSY

There's a problem that you can't figure out. Maybe it's time you stopped turning it over with your conscious mind. It may be time to allow another part of the brain to take over. The right hemisphere of the brain is the part that has the intuitive, instinctual ability to know all at once, without taking each thought through a step-by-step process. In our culture, we favor the left hemisphere with its linear, logical, intellectual approach to problem solving. But not every conclusion can be reached by rational action. When your plan of *action* isn't producing results, perhaps it is time for a plan of *being*.

Some problems need to lie fallow for a period in the same way that a farmer allows the ground to lie fallow for a season. If the farmer works the land without a break, eventually the soil stops yielding. It seems paradoxical, but there comes a point when the land will produce more crops after it has had time to rest and grow nothing. Later, when seeds are planted after this quiet period, the harvest is superb.

Our minds work in the same way.

TODAY'S LESSON:
I will be still and know.

KNOWLEDGE

Education is the key to unlock the golden door of freedom.

—GEORGE WASHINGTON CARVER

At a recent holiday party, people gathered around and told stories about what one person stood out in their lives. Mom and Dad were the most frequently named people, of course. After parents, it was a teacher. And even among people who didn't name a teacher, they named a person whose message was "get an education."

Teachers give a great legacy. We are a Santa Claus who delivers a great gift in daily segments, not just once a year. We give it to the naughty and the nice. Instead of giving a lot of different gifts, toys, and trinkets one day only, we show up all year long with the same precious gift. We present knowledge—the gift that makes the recipient smart, allows him to earn a living, to gain esteem, to prosper in life.

TODAY'S LESSON:

I teach with the awareness that my work is vital.

HUMILITY

A good sport has to lose to prove it.

—ANONYMOUS

Making mistakes is like complaining about the weather. Everybody does it. Teachers make mistakes and sometimes students catch them. Unlike the weather, there is something you can do about it. Do you know what to do when you have wronged a student? Just five words will set it right—"Will you please forgive me?" If five words are too much to fit in your mouth, you can make a four-word statement—"It was my fault." If you can't work your way around that many words, try a two-word sentence—"I'm sorry."

TODAY'S LESSON:

I admit when I'm wrong.

GROWTH

There is no fruit which is not bitter before it is ripe.

—PUBLILIUS SYRUS

Growing pains don't stop once you escape adolescence. If we are to be fully functioning, *no* fully flourishing human beings, we must accept a process of changing and growing that is all too frequently all too excruciating.

Someone once told me that the word "pain" stood for Please Address the Inner Need. Taken in this way, pain is not merely dis-ease but also the pointer to the cure. There is something within us that knows how easily we are willing to be distracted, how quickly we forget to follow through. Pain grabs our attention. Pain is the prelude to change. Do you have the courage to make the change?

TODAY'S LESSON:

I examine the areas of my life that cause me discomfort
and see what lessons they are trying to teach me.

LOVE

The salvation of man is through love and in love.

—VIKTOR FRANKL

One of the mystical things abut teaching is you get to see human nature up close with the covers torn off. Children display the best and worst parts of human nature.

As teachers, we become attuned to the various nuances that reveal what's going on beneath the surface: the talkative child who is not so chatty today, the body language of the eighth grader that suggests he may pick a fight, the blank look on the faces of everyone in the class that lets you know no one "got it." These cues give us meaningful details on how to proceed with wisdom.

These cues are useful when applied to our life outside the classroom, too. When we have an attitude of generosity, grace, and goodwill, streams of information that would otherwise be unavailable open to us.

TODAY'S LESSON:

I try to look at every situation through a lens of love.

RECIPROCITY

Be awful nice to 'em going up, because you're going to meet 'em coming down.

—JIMMY DURANTE

One day, you're going to get pulled over for a ticket, get lost in a strange place, or be sent to the hospital. One day you will be in a situation where you don't know much about what's going on or are experiencing an emergency. One day you will be dependent upon the expertise, the goodwill, or even the mercy of someone you don't know very well.

That someone may be a former student.

TODAY'S LESSON:

I treat students the way I want to be treated.

ACHIEVEMENT

To achieve anything, you must be prepared to dabble on the boundary of disaster.

—STIRLING MOSS

The creators of *Chicken Soup for the Soul* got 123 rejections before a publisher accepted their book. They were told the concept was "too nicey-nice." Since then, more than thirty titles have been generated from this concept with over 53 million copies sold.

Author Alex Haley contemplated suicide, in part because of discouragement about his writing career. He sensed voices telling him that his ancestors were pulling for him to finish the manuscript *Roots*, which he had been struggling to write for nine years. He did so and *Roots* became a best-selling book and remains one of the most watched mini-series in television history.

The Wright Brothers were refused a patent by the Patent Office because nobody believed a machine could actually fly.

The chairman of the board of IBM, Thomas J. Watson, made this statement in 1945—"I think there is a world market for about five computers."

Failure is often inevitable, but it's not irrevocable. After every downfall is the opportunity for uplift. With work, luck, and a little more time, everything could change for the better.

TODAY'S LESSON:
I will not give up on my good idea.

FAILURE

There is the greatest practical benefit in making a few failures early in life.

—T. H. HUXLEY

The sixth-grade poets were primed and ready to compete in a Youth Poetry Slam at a local bookstore. I had a good feeling about the team. These students were motivated and enthusiastic—plus their skills were excellent. I was confident of victory. They were, too.

The average students stepped up to the microphone with authority. The good speakers were stellar. I was proud. The other team was good, too, but that only sharpened the resolve of my team's spirit.

Yet—we lost. Only by a few points, but it was still a defeat. My kids were crushed, both boys and girls left the event sobbing. I knew they were excited about the competition but I had no idea they would take it so to heart.

I decided I needed to do something to console them. I called a veteran teacher to ask her advice. "What should I buy them as a consolation gift?" I asked. "Should it be something for the whole group or maybe some inexpensive item I could give each child?"

"I would buy them nothing," she told me. "They're not too young to learn that this is how life is sometimes. Don't give them a prize for losing. Let them use this as an experience to get better."

The next class we talked about what we had learned from the experience of defeat. The next time we competed, we won.

TODAY'S LESSON:

I am not just teaching academic skills but lessons for living as well.

GOAL SETTING

Sometimes adversity comes in the form of daring to do what's never been done before.

—J. R. REYNOLDS

For some teachers, getting the administrators to listen is the problem. For other teachers, having to listen to administrators is the problem. For some teachers, maintaining discipline is the problem. For others, finding time to try out all the things you'd like to try in the classroom is the problem. For some teachers, lack of community support is the problem. For others, too much outside interference is the problem.

Everyone has problems, but some problems are "higher order" problems. These are issues where the complexity is greater but the potential rewards are also greater. These are problems that are at a deeper level but can move teachers and students to a higher plane.

These are the problems that result not from doing something wrong but from doing something right, something new, or something different. Getting a good idea and putting it into practice is a blessing with a paradoxical edge because when you act on a revelation, you activate a revolution.

TODAY'S LESSON:

I make courageous choices.

ACTION

Do you remember the fable Belling the Cat? The mice were all called to a meeting to discuss how to keep from being attacked by a cat. One mouse suggested tying a bell about the cat's neck. That way, every time the cat approached, the bell would ring and the mice would be warned and be able to run away. "Great idea!" everyone agreed, except for one little detail—who would be the mouse to actually get close enough to put the bell on the cat?

A lot of complaints are levied against the school system—some valid, some vapid, some vicious. Not all the complainers are external to school, either. Teachers have plenty to complain about, too. But we have to put some muscle behind the mouth. Anybody can grumble. But anyone can take action, too.

TODAY'S LESSON:

I am changing the things that need changing.

168

INTEGRITY

Knowing is not enough; we must act, willing is not enough; we must do.

—GOETHE

We already know a lot about what makes education effective. We understand a lot about how children learn. We have been to school ourselves. We have lived life.

We know what to do. Even if we don't know a hundred percent of what to do, we still know plenty.

So do it.

TODAY'S LESSON:

I do not make excuses.

INSTRUCTION

I don't like a man to be too efficient. He's likely to be not human enough.

—FELIX FRANKFURTER

If to the question "What do you teach?" your answer is "geometry," or "computer literacy," or "French," you may want to expand your answer. Yes, we teach a particular subject, but we also teach students. No matter the "what" you teach, it is always secondary to the "who." We do not simply stand up in an empty room writing on the blackboard, typing on a keyboard, or conjugating verbs; we are relating to people, influencing their thoughts, feeding their minds, and hopefully touching their spirits.

TODAY'S LESSON:

I preserve the personal element in my teaching.

GROWTH

The by-product is sometimes more valuable than the product.

—HAVELOCK ELLIS

The average person enters the field of education for one of two reasons: to earn a living or to make a difference. Each of those are honorable reasons. We expect to get a salary and some personal satisfaction in exchange. And most of us get that—plus a few other things we had not bargained for. Working with children reveals aspects of my character, good and bad, that I may not have been in touch with. Teaching underscores the exhilaration of learning and the importance of discipline. Teaching forces me to grow in ways I'd rather not. Teaching forces me to develop patience, and to experience the long-suffering side of love.

Teaching makes me be a better human.

TODAY'S LESSON:

I am willing to do better.

SERENITY

*There comes a point when you really have to spend time with yourself
to know who you are.*

—BERNICE JOHNSON REAGON

Just as it takes hours of drills doing layups before the basketball player can make baskets with ease, just as it takes hours of conversation before closeness is established between friends, just as you spent years in concentrated study to learn your subject content, it takes time spent alone to become comfortable with oneself. Fellowship with friends and meetings with peers are important, but not more important than periods of solitude. Take yourself on a date—plan an hour or two to nurture your soul in the quiet delight of your own company.

You will return to yourself refreshed, renewed, rejuvenated.

TODAY'S LESSON:
I cultivate a good relationship with myself.

HUMILITY

To teach is to learn.

—JAPANESE PROVERB

The more I know, the more I know I don't know. I feel more humble standing before a group of students today than I did the first time I walked into a classroom (and I was plenty nervous that day, too!). The magical thing about teaching is that I continually discover new things about my subject: when students ask me questions I can't answer or point out a slant on a concept I had never considered.

But the most profound learning has come when a situation in the classroom becomes a mirror for my own behavior, when an aspect of my self is reflected and a new side of me is revealed.

TODAY'S LESSON:

I am open to the new truths that present themselves to me today.

COURAGE

Dance as though no one is watching you, love as though you have never been hurt before, sing as though no one can hear you, live as though heaven is on earth.

—UNKNOWN

There are so many things we don't do because . . . of what? Because we may be embarrassed, the neighbors will talk, or our friends will tease us? Is that a good enough reason not to take up ballet, even though you're not rail thin, to give up on love because the last relationship ended on the rocks, or to not enter the contest because there's so much paperwork?

We may no longer have the innocence of a child with huge vistas of opportunities stretched before us, but that does not mean we have no options at all. There is no need to give up the ghost when we still have a willing spirit.

TODAY'S LESSON:

I show up for life.

GROWTH

Blame yourself if you have no branches or leaves. Don't accuse the sun of partiality.

—CHINESE PROVERB

"My—how you've grown!" is what every adult says to any child he or she hasn't seen in more than six months. Because a child's physical growth is rapid, the changes are startling and impressive. You can readily see the difference in Junior's physical stature from year to year.

When was the last time someone said to you, "My—how you've grown"? Not about your physical growth, but growth in intellectual curiosity, moral courage, or victory over your character defects.

Just because we have finished college, raised children, bought a home, or achieved some other milestone in life does not mean we've learned it all. Where wisdom is concerned, there is always room to grow taller.

TODAY'S LESSON:

I challenge myself to excel.

FAIRNESS

They are good, they are bad,
They are weak, they are strong,
They are wise, they are foolish—so am I.

—SAM WALTER FOSS

When I was a child in elementary school, my friends and I used to gripe—we do all the work, but teachers get all the money. *Yeah, right, kid!* Now that I'm on the other side of the desk, I know that teachers have loads of work to do and we earn every penny of the little bit of money we're paid. In fact, now I feel it's the students who have all the advantages; advantages that they don't always appreciate. Teaching has taught me that there's always another side of the desk.

TODAY'S LESSON:

I reserve judgment until I've learned the other side of the story.

GROWTH

There are two kinds of people: those who say to God, "Thy will be done,"
and those to whom God says, "All right, then, have it your way."

—C. S. LEWIS

Folks say there are two ways to quit drinking. One way is to quit drinking. The other way is to keep drinking, for if you keep drinking you will end up in jail, insane, or dead—which will certainly stop you from drinking.

So many of life's lessons are this plain and obvious, yet we avoid facing facts until we back up into a brick wall. If only we were willing to see the light before we feel the heat!

TODAY'S LESSON:

I do not have to learn everything the hard way.

CHAOS

I have great belief in the fact that whenever there is chaos, it creates wonderful thinking.
I consider chaos a gift.

—SEPTIMA POINSETTE CLARK

When you unwrap a fresh deck of cards, all the cards are in perfect sequence, ordered by suit. The ace of hearts through the king of hearts, followed by a sequence of clubs, diamonds, and spades. However, holding a set of cards in perfect order offers no interest or stimulation. The interest comes after the deck has been shuffled, after it has *deliberately* been put in disorder. The challenge and joy of a card game are in putting the cards back into some sort of order, depending on the rules of a given game. Without the shuffle, nothing happens—no excitement, no incentive, no aim. You simply have a sterile, static set of colored cardboard.

Life is a much more intricate and stimulating game than Go Fish or Gin Rummy or even Strip Poker, and the chaotic twists, turns, and upsets that present themselves put much more at stake than a few points on a score card. Teaching, in particular, can be a complicated game when you have to connect with twenty classroom characters, meet all the expectations of the central administration, the school board, and the PTA as well as figure out what to fix for dinner tonight. An "affinity for chaos" should be mentioned in the job description.

But if we can tolerate the chaos, we won't get lost in the shuffle.

TODAY'S LESSON:
I enjoy the game of life.

ENDURANCE

You do not play a sonata in order *to reach the final chord, and if the meanings of things were simply in ends, composers would write nothing but finales.*

—ALAN WATTS

Why hike to the top of a mountain when you can fly to the peak? After all, the view is the same. Or is it?

Of course it isn't. Or rather, the view is the same, but you are different. The climb to the top transforms the climber. The slow progress, the near disaster, the actual disaster, the bonding that develops among your fellow sojourners: These all make their mark on you.

When the only goal is to get to the end, then the end point becomes no different from the beginning because *you* are no different at the end than you were at the beginning. But you don't have to scale Mount Everest to know transformation. Life itself gives you invitations to take the scenic route in your daily affairs: walk instead of drive to run an errand; cook a meal from scratch rather than pop something frozen into the microwave; listen to a child's (or an adult's) rambling explanation rather than cutting him or her off and saying get to the point. Life in and of itself is an adventure that promises peak experiences, if we are willing to appreciate both the ardor and arduousness of the trip.

TODAY'S LESSON:

I'll take the scenic route.

TRUST

Finally, you see that there is nothing you can trust—nobody, no authority—except the process itself.

—A. H. ALMAAS

Nobody knows the answer, at least not the whole answer. No one particular position is absolute, no strategy is right for every situation, no technique is unique.

Teaching is an art and not an exact science. And learning is part magical, part practical—a mystical event. You can trade in your ditto machine for a photocopier, exchange handwritten work for laser-printed documents—and the high-tech approach will produce results—for a while. Then you can revert "back to basics" and do things the old-fashioned way and that will work—for a while.

You can hire technical assistance from the most astute educational experts in the market or accept advice from your grandmother about what will help kids do well in school. And all of that information will work—for a while.

But in the final analysis, if you are committed to teaching, then teach. If you are loving in your approach, whatever that approach is, then trust yourself and the process. If you will to love and mean to teach then your efforts will bear fruit, no matter what the procedure.

TODAY'S LESSON:

I teach, I show love, and I trust the process.

PRIVATE THOUGHTS

Education must have an end in view, for it is not an end in itself.

—SYBIL MARSHALL

PRIVATE THOUGHTS

If you cannot win, make the one ahead of you break the record.

—RICHARD S. ZERA

PRIVATE THOUGHTS

Say nothing about another that you wouldn't want to hear about yourself.

—EL SALVADORAN PROVERB

PRIVATE THOUGHTS

I have proven that children labeled "unteachable" can learn.

—MARVA COLLINS

184

PRIVATE THOUGHTS

When love and skill work together, expect a masterpiece.

—JOHN RUSKIN

PRIVATE THOUGHTS

People see God every day; they just don't recognize him.

—PEARL BAILEY

PRIVATE THOUGHTS

Respect for the rights of others is peace.

—BENITO JUAREZ

PRIVATE THOUGHTS

What's terrible is to pretend that the second-rate is first-rate.
To pretend that you don't need love when you do; or you like your work when
you know quite well you're capable of better.

—DORIS LESSING

PRIVATE THOUGHTS

Do not bear ill will toward those who tell you the truth.

—GUATEMALAN PROVERB

189

PRIVATE THOUGHTS

To be meek, patient, tactful, modest, honorable, brave
is not to be either manly or womanly, it is to be humane.

—JANE HARRISON

PRIVATE THOUGHTS

*There are no problems that we cannot solve together
and very few that we can solve by ourselves.*

—LYNDON JOHNSON

PRIVATE THOUGHTS

There's a deception to every rule.

—HAL LEE LUYAH

PRIVATE THOUGHTS

In the face of uncertainty, there is nothing wrong with hope.

—O. CARL SIMONTON

PRIVATE THOUGHTS

Out of the unforeseen comes the vision.

—W. MORGAN JONES